30.95

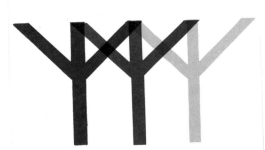

Plants for Shade

Plants for Shade

Allen Paterson

J. M. Dent & Sons Ltd
London Melbourne Toronto

First published 1981
© Text and photographs, Allen Paterson 1981

Printed in Great Britain
by Richard Clay (The Chaucer Press) Ltd, Bungay
for J. M. Dent & Sons Ltd
Aldine House, Welbeck Street, London

This book is set in Linoterm Times 12/14 point by
Oxford Publishing Services

British Library Cataloguing in Publication Data

Paterson, Allen
 Plants for shade.
 1. Shade-tolerant plants — Great Britain
 I. Title
 635.9′54   SB434.7

ISBN 0-460-04419-2

Contents

List of Plates

Acknowledgments

I am indebted to innumerable people, some of whom I have never met, who open their gardens to public view. It is unlikely that anyone grows all the plants described or recommended in this book, and I freely admit that I am no exception. But one cannot really write about plants that one has not seen, hence the grateful acknowledgment made above.

My thanks are also due to Miss Jane Gelder, who nobly typed from my less than impeccable manuscript, and to Miss Lona Mont-Clar, who gave valuable advice on the arrangement of the book.

Allen Paterson   Chelsea Physic Garden
                                                          1980

Preface

'Now I go up into the copse with a man and chopping tools to cut out some of the Scotch fir that are beginning to crowd each other.

'How endlessly beautiful is woodland in winter! Today there is a thin mist; just enough to make a background of tender blue mystery three hundred yards away, and to show any defect in the grouping of near trees. No day could be better for deciding which trees are to come down. . .'

Thus Miss Jekyll in *Wood and Garden* in 1899 — the 'notes and thoughts, practical and critical, of a working amateur'. She was, of course, writing at a time when it was almost inconceivable for a country garden not to have a few acres of woodland adjoining and a few men to run it. And it was Gertrude Jekyll and William Robinson (the above-mentioned book in fact shares some illustrations with the latter's *The English Flower Garden*) who opened the eyes of later nineteenth-century gardeners to the possibility of using hardy plants in ways hitherto undreamt of. The quotation indicates both the literal breadth of the palette with which Jekyll, having perforce because of declining eyesight given up painting, now worked and the depth of her vision of what gardening was about.

The essence of this vision is what all good gardeners develop, the ability to use all situations in the garden to the maximum advantage (even, or indeed especially, when the site or the soil seems to bristle with positive *dis*advantages) and to find in all cases the right plants for the right place concerned.

Such an ability and innate philosophy is nowhere more important than with what is apt to be described in one of the conventional clichés of gardening as 'the problem of shade'.

The following pages are intended firstly to coin a further cliché (for clichés have their value — they repeat the accepted, however wrongly), 'the potential of shade', and secondly to indicate what that potential is.

PART I
The Potential of Shade

One of the great pleasures of gardening lies in that basic promise of a garden — that each is its owner's attempt at creating a personal paradise on earth. This may sound a pretty excessive claim: indeed to suggest to some that man can himself 'create' is little short of apostasy. Yet in the conceiving of what is loved and enjoyed as a whole, in the selection and arrangement of the parts and in the effective cultivation of the plants (itself an extraordinary combination of art and science) we most of us get as close to conscious creation as is ever likely.

The corollary to the fact of a *personal* paradise lies in the fact that every garden is different. The strips of land behind a 1950s housing estate or the necessarily smaller plots behind those in a current development may seem at first sight to possess a daunting similarity, but even before the choice or taste of the owners has been brought to bear basic differences often exist. In the context of this book the immediate difference between two otherwise identical pieces of ground each side of the dividing fence of a pair of conventional semi-detached houses is highly significant. In bigger country gardens with a range of aspects, varying shade and even diversity of soil types, the possibilities of personal individuality are enormous.

It is, then, the effective use of a given site that, in general, makes a good garden. This consists of working with, rather than against, those given facts which exist and which cannot, without excessive expenditure of time or money, if at all, be easily altered. For it seems sensible, as with any other factor of life (and certainly of gardening) to behave positively, to work constructively and to think optimistically about the situations that are to be confronted. Hence the *potential* of shade is here considered a more helpful phrase than that more usual one, the *problem* of shade.

1

The Potential of Shade

It is to be emphasized at once that a garden without shade is a dull place indeed. The word dull is used advisedly; it may be brilliant with the unadulterated rays of the sun but without their opposite, without chiaroscuro, much of their virtue is lost. Successful garden-making, as with any art form, lies in the effective combination and juxtaposition of opposites or dissimilars. The slow movement of a symphony lies between two quick ones, the darkness on one side of a portrait emphasizes the light on the other cheek. The movement of dancing shadows on one side of the garden enlivens the clear sun on the other.

Unlike the sister arts, however, a garden is continually moving. The position of the sun, and therefore the lie of its light, varies from morning to evening and from winter to summer. The plants themselves possess different virtues in these ever changing conditions. The effect produced by tracery of bare branches through which a low winter sun shines is utterly different from that caused by a summer noonday blaze upon the leaves or flowers of the very same plant. They could be separate species as far as their visual impressions are concerned. In woodland, the leaves of the tree canopy, quivering and blowing in the wind, permit sudden increased illumination at ground level, almost as if a light had been suddenly switched on and then, equally suddenly, dimmed. This sort of variation in light concentration is possible, of course, only under living shade (though it is significant that modern technology has produced sunglasses which react similarly to increasing or decreasing sun-strength.) The shade of a building or a garden wall remains shade until the sun gets above it or moves, as the day progresses, round to the side.

Yet although shade of this type from a building may be complete, the actual light concentration at ground level can be relatively high for, unlike ground under the canopy of trees, the sky above is open even if the sun cannot be seen. This is why many tiny town courtyards can be veritable oases of green and flower colour even though they seldom get a glimpse of the sun itself. White- or pale colour-washing of walls and the use of plants with glossy leaves help to capitalize on all the light there is, reflecting it back and forth. Rather as atomic fuel in a nuclear

2

reactor is never used up light is not a consumable commodity: it is always there to the maximum amount that is allowed in.

The phrase used here 'the potential of shade' suggests two particular aspects of garden planning. One refers to making the most of shaded areas which already exist. This offers a whole range of possibilities depending upon each individual site and its features and is considered separately in Chapter 3. The other is that, accepting that a shade-less area lacks much of what makes a garden beautiful, how can shade best be contrived.

1 The Search for Shade

It is generally agreed that the origins of our western European culture lie somewhere, ten thousand years ago or so, in the 'Fertile Crescent' of Mesopotamia. These were areas which even then held water at a premium — or why was the lush greenery of Babylon's Hanging Gardens so extraordinarily remarkable to the contemporary eye that they became known as one of the Wonders of the ancient world?

There followed in other emergent civilizations of the Middle East and later around the Mediterranean littoral, as each people's security became more assured, the development of the arts. Of these the art of garden-making proceeded from early food-producing techniques to highly sophisticated designs reflecting the ideals of the society concerned. Gardens have always embodied the concept of perfection, actual or anticipated ('and the Lord God planted a garden eastward in Eden . . . to grow every tree that is pleasant to the sight, and good for food'). Thus in these areas, whether in Babylon, Egypt, Greece, Rome, Spain or the Riviera, emphasis in gardens was — and to a great extent still is — upon two main factors, water and shade. Both of these in the burning heat of a southern summer are always longed for, combining together as they do to form the archetypal oasis, a paradise. But to make water flow where it had not flowed before or cause trees to grow on inhospitable hillsides is not only paradisal but also an aspect of luxury exemplified: such gardens were (and are) not free from the mere wish to show off, to impress and both to lead and follow fashion.

As in our Christian era the focus of wealth moved from the Renaissance City States of Italy to France and then to Britain, many aspects of the classical world became encapsulated in more northern cultures, as did so much of their languages.

During the two hundred years that centered on the mid-eighteenth century, architects relied almost entirely upon classical precepts and models. So it was in other fields.

In garden design formality at first held sway, based upon Italian and French garden practice of open parterres giving way to allées, bosquets and waterworks — the essence of the well-watered and shaded Elysian fields still catering, in a dull, northern climate, for a hot southern sun. But, as is well known (though the reasons continue to exercise scholars) Britain saw a dramatic change of taste leading to perhaps our one certain contribution to the development of art — *Le Jardin Anglais*. Whether Capability Brown's sweeping away formal layouts and bringing the park to the very doors of the house was a direct product of Addison's pieces in the *Spectator* ('I cannot but fancy that an orchard in flower is not infinitely preferable . . . to the most finished parterre'), or Kent (who 'leapt the fence and saw all nature was a garden') or that great mathematical schemes lost favour because they were French, foreign and frightfully expensive does not really matter. What is significant in the context of this chapter is that, though the climate of Britain in which the new landscaped grounds were being made was in no whit changed, the models were still classical, still Mediterranean.

This time, however, they were based upon the idealized classical scenes of the Roman campagna as depicted by Claude, Poussin and their followers. Examples of these works, brought back by the 'Grand Tourists' of the day, soon began to grace the walls of new or classically re-faced country houses. These took the place, in their own bits of British campagna, of the distant temples seen through Claude's umbrageous views. Other art forms reflect these impressions as well.

It will be remembered that in Handel's opera *Serse* (in English, 'Xerxes, King of Persia') the king of the title is seen as the curtain rises languishing, or about to languish, in a 'Belvedere a canto d'un bellissimo giardino, in mezzo di cui v'e un platano' (i.e. A beautiful garden shaded by a great plane-tree). In an opening recitative he addresses the 'tender boughs' of the tree and then launches into what is universally known as

6

Handel's 'Largo'. The subject of such deep emotion, however, would be a surprise to many music-lovers. The line beginning 'Ombra mai fù' around which the noble tune is built can be simply translated as follows: 'Never was shade cast by any tree more dear'. Only acceptance of the classical ideal of protection from a burning sun can give legitimate meaning to the piece. This extraordinary eulogy of shade (written in Italian and set to music by an expatriot German for an English audience) received its first public performance on 15 April, 1738. It is not at all fanciful to take it as a typical eighteenth-century expectation of the way in which classical figures in a landscape behaved and moved. As in those idealized landscapes of Claude and Poussin of the previous century shade is seen and portrayed as an essential part of any perfect scene, as the obverse of the sunlit coin, each complementing the other, each necessary.

We recall another of Handel's well-known settings, this time from Pope's 'Pastorals':

> Where'er you walk, cool gales shall fan the glade;
> Trees, where you sit, shall crowd into a shade;
> Where'er you tread, the blushing flow'rs shall rise,
> And all things flourish where you turn your eyes.

Here and throughout literature the perfection of shade is shown. Such perfection is, of course, in a contrived landscape or, in other words, a garden.

> Lovely woods with paths dim and silent
> A haunt of peace for weary-hearted
> There's healing in your shade
> and in your stillness balm
> For all who seek repose
>
> (Amadis/Bois Epais, Lully)

Shade as a necessary and expected part of the garden is maintained throughout the literature of the eighteenth century. Cowper's phrase 'Happy Shades' in *The Shrubbery* indicates the way his and other poets' thoughts developed. Though to modern eyes horticulturally dull in the extreme, the Victorian shrubbery provided just the necessary shade and visual protection for gentle dalliance between the heavily overdressed people of that period. Perhaps as the classical images faded shade in the garden became more associated with fashions of dress and appearance: layers of cloth and a milk-white skin need protection when out in the sun. The parasol can only be lowered where trees 'crowd into a shade' otherwise only ex-patriot Englishmen in the company, of course, of mad dogs, went out in the midday sun.

It is at this moment that it is possible to recognize, from a horticultural point of view, the spectre — as yet not more than the cloud over Vesuvius on a fine day — of that dread gardening topic 'The Problem of Shade'. The real problem, however, if there is any problem at all to worry about is that of conventionally expected flowering plants.

The eighteenth century saw no need for plants in great gardens to flower within the broad vistas seen from the house. They appeared in walled kitchen gardens and were available for indoor decoration, while un-fashion-conscious cottage gardens possessed no doubt something of the happy miscellany that ordinary back gardens still possess. The nineteenth century saw the introduction of numbers of exotic flowers which, with the rapidly expanding technology of the time, could be grown under glass and planted out to produce the dazzling displays still to be seen in some seaside resorts. The shrubbery kept to shrubs and a few ubiquitous species of ferns (though often many more in specially arranged ferneries) while the open garden was reserved for carpet bedding. Never, it might have seemed, would the twain have needed to meet. But horticultural innovators such as William Robinson and Gertrude Jekyll recognized an ambiguity here. The shrubbery, with all its dark and gloomy Victorian connotations (so different from, for instance, eighteenth-century Sir Brooke Boothby's comfortably elegant 'chequered shade', as seen in the portrait by Joseph Wright of Derby) offered in fact great possibilities for the growing of many admirable plants which actually liked shade. This fact was emphasized by the artificiality of the carpet-bedding craze.

In many cases the plants were already to hand: 'American' plants (usually synonymous with calcifuge or lime-hating

shrubby species) had already had some keen adherents particularly at the beginning of the century and, as it progressed
further plants of this type from the Old and New World were
brought in. Also a mid-nineteenth-century enthusiasm for a
diversity of hardy ferns brought some use to the shadier parts of
the garden (consciously planted or naturally so).

Perhaps had society stayed static the plantsmanship of
Robinson and Jekyll and other early twentieth-century innovators would have ensured that the traditional parts of the
garden, open and shaded, would have remained equally necessary and equally used. But society and fashion do not remain
static.

Several trends can be traced. As the twentieth century
progressed, with the problems of obtaining and affording good
paid help, gardens tended to become smaller. The once expected progression of terraces giving way to lawns, merging
into woodland (natural or contrived) with separate gardens for
specific groups of plants ceased to be possible. Obviously many
great gardens continued, and fortunately, still continue. A few
new gardens on the grand scale continue to be made. But the
diminution is inevitable and inexorable and no direct concern of
this book. Except that with changes in garden styles has come,
in parallel, a change in what people do in gardens. Decorous tea
taken in formal dress under the necessary shade of the deodar
on the lawn may still occur when the vicar comes to call (the
association is inescapable; *Cedrus deodara* was, par excellence,
a vicarage lawn tree — a Victorian ballad celebrates the fact).
More commonly now alfresco meals are taken in full sun beside
a swimming pool with a minimum of clothing.

It seems then that we have moved into a new age of helios-
worshippers whose acolytes are trained at various coeduca-
tional seminaries labelled 'Clubs Mediterranées'. So dominant
has this 'liberated' attitude become that it permeates a surprising number of aspects of contemporary life, not always to
their benefit. Glass walls of office blocks and public buildings
need immediate internal shading, 'picture windows' (often with
no picture in view but the opposite identical window across the
road) in new housing estates have immediately to be draped in a

multiplicity of curtains for privacy and protection from the sun. For shade, it seems, is still necessary, and still enjoyed.

Most importantly, it is enjoyed by a large number of beautiful garden plants which succeed best, last longer and look best in the conditions for which they are particularly adapted. The ecological background to such development is considered in Chapter 2.

2 Shade Plants in the Wild

For any living organism, plant or animal, to succeed it must be in some equilibrium with its surroundings. It is part of the food-chain or food-web by which numbers of highly dissimilar creatures are connected: it feeds, it is fed upon. To be there, to have developed, indicates that it has properties and adaptations that make it successful in its chosen habitat. But 'chosen' is altogether too anthropomorphic a word: a mole has not *chosen* to live underground any more than a water-lily has *chosen* to live in a pond. They are organisms which, in response to pressures of competition and space, have managed to move into an otherwise under-used ecological niche. To do so, over evolutionary time, they have made morphological adaptations which fit them ideally for such niches, just as they are unfitted for anything else. Above ground lack of effective sight would be highly disadvantageous to a mole just as lack of strengthening tissue makes a high and dry waterlily a poor thing indeed.

It is worth while keeping such general thoughts in mind when considering the broader aspects of the ways in which plants grow in the wild, because although our own garden palette may be almost entirely based upon man-bred cultivars, these are in fact still very close to their wild ancestors, and hence their needs do not differ markedly from what these forbears became adapted for, and then could not manage without. This is significant when considering plants for shade and woodland situations.

Firstly we should consider the basic facts of that branch of biology known as plant ecology. Ecology may be defined simply as the study of plants in the wild. It is not therefore primarily concerned with the cell structure of plant species (as is cytology) or formal relationship (as is taxonomy) or even with the way the plant works (as is physiology) — though it is bound to be concerned with the interaction of these and other branches of botany. For it is such interaction within individual plants which makes them interact with each other and makes possible, in response to the external factors of climate and soil, the typical aspects which we recognize when passing through any bit of countryside.

In Britain a relatively short motorway journey will take us through several distinctive types. Through chalk downland, perhaps (recent road cuttings help diagnosis no end); later, in the valley, woodland takes over and subsequently pine and heather indicate an area of heathland. Even to a casual ob-server — preferably *not* the driver: botanizing at speed is not to be recommended — the vegetation, even if not identified, is different. The sparse yews and juniper, with traveller's joy clambering about, present a very different impression from the thicker canopy in the clay vale or the broad sweeps of purple heather on the moors.

Each of these areas has its own particular plant communities which make up clearly recognizable units of vegetation. Throughout the world such distinct communities, often highly diverse, can be found. The *maquis* of the Mediterranean is a community of tough thorny shrubs protecting an understory of early-flowering herbaceous plants. In the jungle of the Amazon headwaters great trees, lianas, epiphytes and eventually terres-trial species combine to form an equally typical, though utterly different, community.

Within each community, however, there are usually smaller recognizable plant groups in which one type of plant is the most noticeable and which has something of an overbearing effect upon its fellows. This is the dominant species or, if there are more than one, the co-dominant. Such a group is called a plant association and any number of associations make up a plant community.

Because we are here concerned with shade-tolerant plants it would be suitable to take a bit of damp oak woodland, which can still be found in many parts of northern Europe, to illustrate these ecological terms. In doing so something of the lives of woodland plants can be discovered.

Here, pedunculate oak (*Quercus robur*) is the big dominant tree, in the shade of which grow hazel, bramble and honeysuckle. Below these are herbaceous species, woodspurge, primrose, ground-ivy, violet and self-heal. Lower still, both in stature and evolutionary order, are mosses, a liverwort or two and algae. Such a community will not be constant, for where shade is less dense or availability of soil moisture or nutrient varies clear associations develop. Herbaceous woodspurge may be dominant in any one area over a number of less frequent species and we could refer to this sub-unit as a woodspurge association.

It is obvious that what is being described is the layered effect of natural vegetation or, as it is usually described, its stratification. Leave any area of soil free, even in the middle of the biggest town, and plants will take over, gradually building up to the community of plants that is natural to that area (or as near natural as is possible: in London for example the availability of acorns to provide the eventual oak tree layer which has been displaced by two thousand years of man's activities may be replaced by sycamore or plane, with subsequent differences in the lower layers because the humus formed by fallen leaves would be different). London without man would revert to woodland, however composed.

Such a contingency, except in the inflated imaginations of science fiction writers is, hopefully, not likely to occur. But in the country it does. A marvellously documented example of this is at Rothamsted Agricultural Research Station, where small areas of land have been consciously left naturally to regenerate from ploughland to Hertfordshire woodland. The process is predictable.

First appear the small-seeded annual garden weeds: their seeds may have been dormant for decades or recently blown in. Their rapid life-cycle will soon be repeated but by the end of the first year some plants are clearly going to overwinter. Such herbaceous perennials are soon joined by shrubs — blackberry or hawthorn — as birds coming to collect seeds leave the pips of fruits they had elsewhere earlier consumed. In the protection of these bushes tree seedlings grow into saplings and emerge above them, the speed of such regeneration depending upon soil nutrients and weather and perhaps animals. Meanwhile, of course, the annuals have been crowded out and, no bare soil being available, further germination is impossible. Shortly, too, the earlier perennial colonizers will lack the space and full sun they initially enjoyed and they also have to move on. Eventually, then, a climax community fully adapted to the competition, the climate and the soil has developed, and settles into the equilibrium mentioned at the beginning of this chapter. No doubt such apparent calm is only relative and this description is a gross over-simplification of what is in fact a highly complicated and sophisticated series of interactions. What is important, however, in the context of shade-tolerant plants for the garden is the realization that the best of these plants are those which, as products of such natural successions over millions of years, are programmed to succeed in just such a situation.

It is worthwhile examining the behaviour of woodland as it affects the plants in the lower levels and also to consider the different types of natural woodland, because each encourages its own type of understory and, in a garden sense, permits a different range of introduced plants.

Deciduous woodland as we know it is very much a western European speciality. A temperate climatic zone with a marked but not excessively prolonged cold season is typical almost exclusively in the northern hemisphere with the exception of certain mountainous districts of New Zealand and South America (these might well produce useful garden plants for us). In all areas with a marked winter plants have to come to terms with low temperatures. In temperate zones most herbaceous plants go underground and trees survive by dropping their leaves and becoming semi-dormant: the deciduous habit is obligatory — a product of evolutionary adaptation to habitat. Even if grown under glass deciduous trees will colour and shed their leaves just as if they were outside.

What triggers this off is still not fully explained but day length must have some close effect because each species goes through the process over a very short span regardless of where grown. And almost regardless of the weather in any given year in Britain we know that we should visit Westonbirt Arboretum for the autumn colour (though quality may vary from year to year) in about the third week in October. To enjoy the spectacular colours of the fall in Vermont, U.S.A. the dates are even clearer.

It should be remarked in passing that many trees in tropical forests do become deciduous while not being typical deciduous trees. Their habit is a facultative leaf-shedding which is less seasonal and not necessarily annual but caused by the tree/soil water balance being upset by drought, and an emergency transpiration reduction becomes necessary. And how better to do this than by shedding those organs through which water-loss occurs? Conversely there are very few evergreen broad-leaved plants of north temperate woodlands. In Britain they can be listed on fewer than the fingers of one hand: holly, ivy, box, *Daphne laureola* — the last two are pretty uncommon at that. All must be seen as being on the northern limit of their range, and they get so far north only because of the modifying influence of the Gulf Stream Drift and of being on the western side of a great continental landmass.

The shorter summer (and longer winter) to the north and east, in alpine regions of continental Europe and most of North America, encourages evergreen conifers. Their needle-like leaves are very resistant to winter cold and also to water loss (referred to as being xeromorphic). They are thus present to photosynthesize very early in spring and exploit the short summer to greatest effect. Larch, incidentally, though deciduous, manages to succeed with a high productivity made possible by the long days of a far northern summer.

But our broad-leaved deciduous trees, and the exotic deciduous species we grow from all over the temperate world, need a warm vegetative season of at least four to six months. Leaves which open anew each spring must have a photosynthetic season ahead long enough to build up extension growth, buds and flowers as well as to set ripe fruit to reproduce the species. Adequate moisture during the growing season is also vital: in western and central Europe north of the Alps it is pretty evenly distributed throughout the year. In eastern North America and eastern Asia (also areas of deciduous forest if not too far north) the maximum rain comes in summer.

Because the tree species have become adapted to succeed in such conditions by becoming leafless for nearly half the year other species have opportunely taken on the role of filling the time gap: indeed there is otherwise little chance in dense woodland for them to do so. They must get on with their own life-cycles while there is light enough to photosynthesize, without which green plants cannot exist. While adequate moisture, nutrients, warmth, oxygen and carbon dioxide (four essentials for plant growth) are generally present only the equally vital illumination rapidly decreases as spring gets into its stride. This is the season of woodland floor plants.

Obviously the amount of light reaching the forest floor, or the herbaceous plants growing there, depends not only on the species but upon the general age of the species which is dominant. For example young forest in full leaf lets very little light down and this is especially marked in beechwoods. Here is a tree species which grows in unusually pure stands (it must be realized that there is very little truly wild woodland, entirely unmanaged, in Britain or indeed western Europe). A walk taken through such a wood in high summer is an almost eerie experience: the smooth elephant-grey trunks stretch up to an unbroken canopy of pale green. The analogy with a cathedral of Gothic cluster-columns is not too fanciful when associated with the quiet and shut-in calm — even the wind seems a long way off, and at one's feet, almost like the strewing herbs of medieval times, a rustling carpet of dry, undecomposed leaves. There are virtually no other plants. Only towards the woodland's edge where light increases is there any clear herbaceous layer — even here orchids such as Bird Nest (*Neottia nidus-avis*), which is a saprophyte and hence not dependent upon its own photosynthetic powers, are apt to occur.

The dramatic drop in light availability at the beechwood floor has been measured: Mid-May, 6 per cent; one week later, 3 per cent; 7 June 1·5 per cent. The diversity in herbaceous species is aided in oak woods or woods with one or more co-dominants. The more open canopy can give surprising bursts of light as branches move in the wind or as the sun travels across the sky; rays and flecks of light can raise the illumination on lower plants by 10–30 per cent, if only in short bursts. Even without such unpredictability a Central European oak-hornbeam forest has given the following figures, 12 March, 52 per cent; 15 April, 32 per cent; 10 May, 6·4 per cent; 4 June, 3·7 per cent.

It should not be surprising therefore that woodland floor plants — even some of the woody ones — begin their seasonal growth very early indeed. Yet surprised one always is. Every year, gathering holly in an English mixed wood for Christmas decoration, we are apt to remark on how the bluebells are sprouting and that the honeysuckle has fresh rosettes of leaves. And this on the shortest day or near to it. But to those plants there is as much useful light as in high summer and they have got to move ahead or perish. They come into flower in spring, the time of primroses, bluebells and solomon's seal and as the tree canopy develops the herbaceous layer yellows and rests; its autumn starts in June.

It is clear therefore that there is a microclimate on the woodland floor vastly different from that in the open meadow beyond. Light is not the only difference. Temperature is more moderate, cooler in summer and milder in winter. Even though tree canopy intercepts over 10 per cent of rainfall, the humidity of the air at ground level, having protection from wind, is higher. The upper layers of the soil are quicker to warm up (the slow leafing of trees is to some extent explained by the coldness of the deeper levels of soil where most of their roots lie). It is interesting to note that many woodland floor plants appear as open-ground species at higher altitudes where similar humidity can be obtained.

But it is not all gain. In periods of drought, trees, with their higher cell-sap salt concentrations, have a greater 'pull' on the available moisture and with it, especially on shallow soils, take much of the available plant nutrients. In such cases the usual root-layer stratification, which may be seen as something of a mirror image of what is above ground, fails to occur. How wise

17

then that the herbaceous layer goes to rest before the battle begins: the fact that so many forest floor plants have evolved storage organs is significant. Bulbs, corms and tubers are vital for surviving the inclement summer period as well as for increasing the species by vegetative means. The production of seeds must always be seen as problematical and the barren strawberry (*Potentilla sterilis*) is one woodlander which has quite given up the struggle. Most plants, however, maintain their fight; eventually in the wild even the noblest forest giant crashes to the ground taking others with it and opening up a wide glade for regeneration to begin, from annual to oak tree, all over again.

3 Shade, Shade Plants and the Site

Effective gardening in a very specialized and sophisticated way does resemble the natural colonization of a site by plants just described. For it is concerned not simply with plants that are loved, admired or coveted but more importantly with choosing the right plants for the right place and, therefore, in the context of this book to be using shade-loving or shade-tolerant plants effectively. There are two aspects to this. One, obviously, is to grow on north walls, in north-facing borders, in shady court-yards of whatever aspect, or under trees and shrubs those species which accept or enjoy the position because, as has already been explained, they are evolutionarily adapted to something similar in their natural habitat. The second is to find places for plants which, because of their inherent beauty (and, it must be realized, eyes of beholders are proverbially dis-similar) cannot be left out and which need shade. These may be, to mention but a few shade-loving herbaceous things, candel-abra primulas, trilliums, *Smilacina racemosa*, and meconopses. The list of exquisite plants could go on (and, in subsequent chapters, will).

In desiring to grow such plants the possibilities (or capa-bilities as the famous Mr Lancelot Brown was apt to describe them in the eighteenth century) of each site must be discovered and exploited to the full. Actual lack of full exposure to the sun is not the only criterion. Growing plants are a product of their garden's soil, moisture availability, general climate, micro-climate (which the plants themselves affect and help to make) as well as aspect.

In general the type of garden soil has two main facets which affect our choice of plants. These are moisture availability and acidity or alkalinity.

Soil water can be considered as being present in two ways. In addition to the water table it is held as a film around every soil particle and thus its amount will be determined by the size of these particles. Soil particles, which are made by the weathering of rock forms and subsequently moved and laid down by the action of glaciation, water and so on, are of many types. Because of their quantity the smallest, those of clays, hold around them a larger amount of water than the bigger sand particles. So much so indeed that clay soils are, to a gardener, wet and heavy to work and often with a completely saturated water table not far down. Paradoxically, in spite of much water being present, in periods of drought plants growing in very heavy clays often find it difficult to raise the water for their use.

Sandy soils, on the other hand, hold little moisture — though what exists is usually freely available — are easy to work and are quick to warm up in spring. Of course what most of us have is something less extreme, with a mixture of sand and clay particles, the proportion of each causing the soil to tend towards one type or the other. Few unfortunately enjoy that fabled recommended desideratum of so many plants 'a deep, rich medium loam well-drained yet retentive of moisture'.

What differences of soil moisture-holding capacity mean, in the context of this book, is the ability to grow woodland plants not only in soils ameliorated by centuries of leaf-fall but in non-woodland conditions as well. In evolving to succeed in shade most species have relatively large leaves to capitalize upon what light they can catch. Little concern has to be given to moisture retention because wind and exposure does not occur, so that water loss is not much of a problem. Out of this context woodlanders demand a consistently moist soil and this, if its structure is improved by copious addition of humus (compost, leaf-mould, spent hops, very well-rotted manure and so on) a clay soil can offer.

Even here, however, full southern exposure without mid-day shade, or a windy position, will be unacceptable — and anyway, to repeat the vital adage of 'the right plant in the right place', such a spot calls for plants that actually enjoy the conditions. But it does mean that east or west aspects as well as the entirely shaded north-facing borders can offer highly acceptable homes to many lovely woodland plants. Not surprisingly plants used to cool shade will have a shorter flowering season if they spend even half their day in sun and petals of the most susceptible may bleach or burn.

It is here that northern gardeners have a great advantage: the high rainfall and more moderate sun makes possible the use of many southern shade-lovers as normal open-garden plants. The habitat range of the plants in a good Scottish herbaceous border is often a lesson in unlikely ecological associations.

While it is comforting to realize that the groans of the clay-soil gardener can be moderated by emphasizing its potential in this way, those of us on the lighter sands (smugly winter-digging with ease even after heavy rain) need also to search out the inherent potential in summer as well because the disadvantages are only too clear. Sunnier aspects will encourage Mediterraneans, South Africans and Californians of all types of perennation form from ephemeral annuals to shrubs. But to vary the garden scene and to capitalize upon the site, shady borders under a north wall or against the house may be the only possible home not only for woodlanders but moisture-lovers too, which would stand no chance in the open garden here.

The basic physical adaptations to habitat which woodland plants have to adopt have been mentioned already more than once. There is also a chemical aspect, which affects our choice of species, and cannot be neglected. It is of course the fact of soil acidity or alkalinity (liminess) which cuts such a swathe through any hopeful, but uninformed, perusal of nurserymen's catalogues.

If the type of soil is not immediately apparent from what grows naturally on the site or in other nearby gardens — one really healthy rhododendron is a clear indicator of an acid soil — it is essential that it be tested. The answer is given on what is referred to as the pH scale. This runs from 1–14 with 7 as the mid and hence neutral point, and simple kits are available which by colour-coding give a perfectly adequate guide.

Any reading above 7 indicates a concentration of lime which makes virtually impossible the growing of several large groups of highly desirable shade-loving or shade-tolerant plants, including particularly virtually all members of the *Ericaceae* family (rhododendrons, azaleas, heathers etc.). Conversely, figures below pH 7 not only permit these groups but do not militate against any lime-tolerant species — though the kitchen garden may have trouble with cabbages.

In practice pH 4·5 is the lowest likely to be experienced, in very acid conditions, and pH 8·5 above pure chalk. Ideally, were one able to choose the 'deep rich loam' etc., it would also have a pH of 6·5 to cater for every possible vegetable taste.

The determining factors of soil pH are several but in brief the origin of the soil's parent rock and subsequent plant deposition are most significant. Old igneous rocks and sandstone are most likely to give acid-reacting soils, and limestones and chalk soils have a high pH. Clays and sands, depending on their origin, can be of either type and, most importantly, can be varied by long periods of plant growth

Centuries of leaf-fall and accumulations of other plant remains have a naturally acid reaction. It is extreme in situations of poor drainage where anaerobic conditions produce peat. More normally bacteria and fungi break down the organic material almost at the rate at which it falls and the leaf-mould in mature woodland indicates the sort of material and its amount which develops. Although not very acidic by comparison with peat or moorland soils, such organic matter is likely to have a pH reading below 7 even when the woodland is growing over limestone or chalk.

In the wild this will be indicated by patches of calcifuge (lime-hating) species, which often appear at variance with the surrounding vegetation, and in woodland gardens especially by the presence of ericaceous plants. Attempts to create artificially acid woodland conditions unblessed by time are invariably doomed to failure — except on the smallest scale, though raised beds of imported lime-free soil in a courtyard situation can often be admirable. These will be discussed further.

What is obvious, therefore, from this discussion is that woodland plants, which make up so large a proportion of our garden shade-lovers, shrubs, herbaceous flowering plants and ferns alike are adapted to growing in organic soils with an acid reaction of greater or lesser concentration. Successful cultivation depends, as always, on reproducing as nearly as possible the conditions the chosen plants find ideal. This will differ with the site and the type of shade being afforded. Is it from buildings or from trees?

This last needs consideration. Anyone coming to a garden soon after the house is finished being built will soon discover that there seem to be almost as many bricks under the soil as appear above it. This is nowhere more true than in the borders under the walls of the house itself (which borders, hopefully, actually exist: what marvellous sites for growing plants of all types are wasted when the base of walls meet not soil but a sea of concrete). For shade-loving plants the obvious aspects will be used, and in an otherwise shadeless garden the opportunities for large-leaved, architectural things are invaluable. The bigger Hostas, *Rheum palmatum* and Rodgersias will contrast splendidly with vertical-leaved *Iris pseudacorus* 'Variegata' or *Phormium tenax*.

But for such garden pictures, shade must be complemented by a humus-rich soil, which is almost certainly not present. Building works bring to the surface subsoil, often virtually inert as a plant-growing medium — even though a thin layer of carefully spread top soil may initially obscure the dread fact. Lumps of impervious clay and other unpleasantness will have to be removed entirely and the whole border brought up to scratch, literally.

The initial alkaline reaction of both mortar and concrete should not be forgotten if calcifuge species are planned, so that peat and acid leaf-mould will be necessary to maintain a below-7 pH reading even on soils that would have been naturally thus. Where this problem is thought to be considerable a dressing of 2–3 oz. of flowers of sulphur to each square yard of border, forked in at least a month before planting, will help. Naturally limy soil is of course accepted but to increase the humus level is equally vital.

However, having been well prepared, house borders need cause little subsequent problems: a balance will need to be kept between the climbers and other wall-plants and the low shrubs and herbaceous plants at their feet. But because of their very nature competition is unlikely to be a great problem.

Such, unfortunately, is not always the case when planting under trees. Established open woodland with a high canopy — the sort of perfect site that in any ideal world none of us would be without — needs little said about it. The shade-tolerant species will settle down in the leaf-mould like a hen on her nest. Far more common is the situation where a tree or two call for underplanting or where, it being the only place, shade plants are going to be grown, come hell or high water, as the saying goes. It is, however, not very apposite: low water would be nearer the mark.

Individual trees may well not be the ideal deep-rooted oaks but have shallow and rapacious root-systems which can seem to gobble up everything you put in for the herbaceous plants, like a flock of starlings on the bird-table taking food meant for blue-tits. Each site and each tree will need its own treatment and it must be realized that under some trees little will grow unless much effort is put into the remedy.

Obviously if one feeds the soil under a tree (a single specimen seldom builds up much leaf-mould underneath it) with organic material or inorganic fertilizers, and provides more water in times of drought, it will respond by increased growth both above and below ground. Neither is likely to help the shade-lovers underneath. Thus a conscious programme of branch-thinning (not pollarding or irresponsibly cutting back) should go hand in hand with root-pruning to attempt to balance the situation — careful reduction of root or crown reduces growth in the other. In some cases it may be worthwhile to excavate the soil for a foot or so to where the tree roots are omnipresent and to lay a perforated plastic membrane and irrigation pipes before returning the (improved) soil. This certainly helps to retain moisture and to prevent tree roots taking more than their share but it is difficult to avoid a feeling of artificiality. Generally it is better to accept the possible and make the most of that, rather than to fight a rearguard action every inch of the way. One could, as a last resort, always move.

Reference has already been made to shade from walls and

buildings where the situation is very different from that shade afforded by trees. It is at once more permanent yet, through lack of an overhead canopy, less dense. Close in the lee of high-rise buildings, as with the denser evergreen trees, sun may never penetrate at all, yet this in no way means that highly effective planting cannot succeed.

Every ordinary detached house — or garden shed for that matter — offers, in the simplest analysis, four basic aspects. Perhaps they may be considered as the sun meets them, or fails to, as the seasons and the days progress. The variation is considerable and becomes more marked as one progresses to the poles from the equator. At the equator, of course, there is no differentiation of season, with perpetual (and ultimately very boring) summer being experienced at lowland levels and in the mountains such extraordinary daily variation as to make the inhabitants of Quito in Ecuador (at 9,000 ft (3 km.) the highest capital city in the world) assert that their climate progresses through the seasons each day: in the morning it is like spring, noonday is high summer, autumn comes by late afternoon and a wintry night follows. Permanent shade in such conditions is particularly difficult to deal with.

In our north-temperate countries things are very different. Seasons are marked, inexorable yet usually relatively gentle in their progressions — though of course weather, as distinct from climate, produces records every year. Day length too, enormously significant to plant growth and flowering, is highly variable. Southern Britain at latitude 45°N experiences nearly a sixteen hour day for a few weeks each side of midsummer day while northern Scotland enjoys perhaps twenty hours. This may be of little significance to humans who insist upon their eight hours of nightly sleep, but it extends plants' photosynthetic time for as long as illumination lasts.

The other side of the coin, inevitably, is extremely short winter days but to plants adapted to the regime that such a climate entails this is of remarkably little importance as they are by then in winter dormancy

The significance of such day-length and seasonal variation to the shade produced by an isolated building will be obvious.

25

The farther north in latitude one goes the more of the northern sky is used by the sun and hence an even north-facing wall will get sunshine on it early in the morning. Successionally, therefore, an east wall will be lit until noon, the southern aspect enjoys full sun for towards half the day. At the end of the western exposure the north wall again gets an hour or two of low sun. All of this, obviously, must be kept in mind if each aspect is to be most effectively used.

4 Trees for Shade

In any new garden one naturally wishes to possess the on-going beauty of trees. Their 'weight' and height is essential to give scale to buildings: they enhance good architecture, both old and new, and ameliorate that which is mediocre or downright bad. They also create shade. As a specimen lawn tree the depth of shade may not be particularly important; on the hottest days, even though we are no longer dressed in Victorian black bombazine or serge, complete sun-protection is still welcome. The wine stays cool at lunch and the butter does not run off the dish at tea. The old phrase 'grateful shade' comes to mind.

In such a spot any tree which is considered beautiful, evergreen or deciduous, broad-leaved or coniferous, is suitable. The grass will not be particularly good; in winter it may almost disappear but *Poa annua* will bulk it up again in summer when it is most wanted.

Choice of trees to produce shade especially for growing the lovely woodland plants that a fully sunny garden finds impossible is, however, a different matter. The perfect species, perhaps, has not been invented. But it is possible to list the desiderata and choose those which come nearest to the ideal.

Firstly, of course, as the biggest plants around, the shade-giving trees must be beautiful in their own right. (As with the oft-quoted definition of equality, all trees are beautiful but some are more beautiful than others. Much.) They should come into leaf late and drop their leaves relatively early to give the ground-level plants a maximum of illumination at times when they are (as evolved woodlanders) at the particularly important periods of their life-cycles. Hence they will not be evergreen. And the higher the canopy the better they develop.

The trees' habit should be open with rather small leaves to permit a modicum of summer light for summer-growing woodland-edge plants to succeed. And, as underground parts of plants are likely to show a similar stratification to those above, deep-rooted trees leave the upper layers of soil free for the roots of shrubs and herbaceous plants. Lastly they should not harbour pests or diseases which affect the species below.

Such requirements make certain lovely trees unsuitable for a mixed garden community. The woodland floor under naturally growing beechwoods is bare: their canopy is so utterly effective — for *them*. Anything left under common limes in summer, whether it is a car or a baby in its pram, gets covered in sticky honeydew. Both of those prized possessions can be washed but plant leaves hold it long enough for subsequent growth of unsightly sooty moulds to develop. The fallen leaves of planes and horse-chestnuts are of such a size as to damage semi-resting herbaceous plants unless raked off quickly.

While the list of unsuitable trees could continue, it is more productive to consider those which can be recommended to provide slight shade. With the Mount Etna Broom (*Genista aetnensis*) it is possible to have tree height in a small garden with virtually no shade at all, because it is leafless — hence invaluable in a site already shaded at ground level by walls. *Genista patula* and tamarisk can do the same job though they are less elegant unless pruned with care.

Of forest-sized trees (and it should be emphasized that small to medium-sized gardens can frequently benefit from bigger trees than are often permitted), the birches are in many ways ideal. It is sensible to use the plural because lovely though our own 'Lady of the Woods' is (the common silver birch, *Betula pendula*) there are several others which should be considered. *Betula pendula* 'Tristis' is taller than the type with delicate weeping branches. The Swedish birch is rather similar and equally beautiful.

From farther east come the lovely *Betula jacquemontii*, with brilliantly white trunks, and *Betula ermanii*, taller, and with pinkish bark. All these birches are splendid light-shade-givers and their lovely trunks are enhanced by careful associations of shade-tolerant plants beneath. Much of the beauty of birches in the wild lies in their frequently irregular growth. Gardeners are not foresters, to whom gnarled and crossing trunks are, under-standably, anathema. Thus the conventional straight standard tree is often best replaced by a multi-stemmed specimen. If this is not available from the nursery (and such a conception is slow in catching on in this country) three to five young plants — seedlings a couple of years or so old — can be carefully planted in one hole. Mutual competition will cause growth to lead outwards and a beautiful 'single' plant with several trunks will develop.

A similar growth pattern can be encouraged in other light-shade trees. If a deep moist soil is available *Cercidiphyllum japonicum* is a good choice — though not in areas subject to late spring frosts. To fine shape and texture are added varying autumn colours as an annual, if unpredictable, bonus.

Other trees offer spring flowers such as the small-leaved magnolias, for example *Magnolia kobus*, *Magnolia salicifolia* and *Magnolia × loebneri* (the latter is perfectly happy on chalk). So too do the more delicate crab apples and cherries. In almost all cases the wild species, if not so dramatic in their floral display, are more suitable for this particular garden role. They include *Malus toringoides* and *Malus transitoria* and *Prunus subhirtella* (the winter cherry is one of its forms and ideal above summer-flowering shade-lovers because its area thus offers interest for twelve months of the year). Closely related is the delicate *Amelanchier canadensis*. Much bigger but excellent for the job is our native cherry, *Prunus avium*. The flowers are rather fleeting but autumn colour adds another . season of value.

Good too are the mountain ashes — species of *Sorbus* of the *Aucuparia* section. These have elegant ferny leaves, very dis-tinct from the heavier foliage of the white beam-type members of the genus. Young plants of our wild mountain ash can be turned into multi-stemmed specimens as described for birches. Again, the effect is so much more attractive than a straight nursery-stock standard standing to attention.

For small gardens other good shade trees are *Styrax japonica* — lime-free soil is essential — some of the maples such as *Acer negundo* 'Variegatum', *Acer griseum* and the snake barks *Acer davidii* and *Acer grosseri*, and although common the not-to-be-despised stag's-horn sumach *Rhus typhina*. This is small, little more than a shrub, but of true trunk-and-branch tree shape and very suitable for the smallest shade garden.

For the obvious reason of encouraging the early growth of the woodland floor species which are a part of this exercise in garden picture-making all trees so far recommended are deciduous. Deep, dark evergreens would be out of place but a very few are light enough in effect and shade production to be acceptable in this role. In mild areas the ferny-leaved mimosa, whose powder-puffs of scented yellow flowers are so welcome in February and March, is one such. The delicate-leaved *Azara microphylla* — also an early spring flowerer smelling this time of vanilla — is somewhat hardier but is still not a plant for cold areas. (As a guide it might be worth mentioning that there is — or was — a good open ground specimen in the University Botanic Garden at Cambridge which, climatically, is hardly Madeira.) One or two gums too could be considered, such as *Eucalyptus gunnii* (the hardiest), *Eucalyptus niphophila* and *Eucalyptus pauciflora*. One suitable group of evergreen shade-providers, of undoubted hardiness, is *Cotoneaster* × *watereri* and its relations. Though usually considered as shrubs their vigour is such that they can be pruned up into delicate open-topped small trees. Their berrying effect is dramatic.

Where space permits the creation or development of a woodland garden proper, forest-sized trees will obviously be used. Birches and *Prunus avium* will still be valuable for their own particular virtues but it is now possible to consider other species. As can be seen from even a cursory examination of natural woodland, oaks are ideal shade trees. They permit rich understories of shrubs and herbaceous plants, their fallen leaves make the best leaf-mould, their roots are deep and thus compete less greedily than most other trees. But it must be admitted they are slow to build up a crown. Hence, no doubt, they must be combined with other quicker yet more transient species. Few exotic oaks can compare with the 'English Oak' (*Quercus robur*) but others of interest and beauty include the chestnut-leaved oak and the various red oaks from North

America. There, in the south-eastern states, tulip trees and sweet gums (*Liquidambar*) share woodlands with certain native oaks and permit a forest floor flora of extraordinary richness. Such use in western Europe is obviously equally possible: the species do well here although they are apt to be considered solely (and unnecessarily) as specimen lawn trees.

Frequently in the garden situation only one full-sized tree is possible to produce shade. Many of the previously mentioned species are suitable (multi-stemmed again) but their number can be added to by plants which develop a distinctive outline when grown alone. Amongst the best is *Koelreuteria paniculata*, the Willow Pattern or Goldenrain Tree. The former vernacular name (although of course Willow Pattern plates are an English eighteenth century confection in the Chinese taste and the romantic story which goes with them a nineteenth-century superimposition) admirably indicates its mature shape: unlike many trees, however, it begins to assume it at a relatively early age.

Good too, and very easy to grow, is a false-acacia, *Robinia*, and its close relative the honey-locust (*Gleditsia triacanthos*), both with typical ferny leaves. Other small-leaved trees for this role are *Zelkova, Celtis* (the hackberries) and *Nothofagus* (the southern beeches) now being widely tried here. In a cold spot, even on difficult heavy soil, common ash is admirable and larch, a deciduous conifer, deserves to be much more often considered as a garden tree. Few plants have such refreshing spring leaves nor such clear yellow autumn ones. Eventually too the shape of a mature larch grown as a specimen is magnificent.

PART II
The Plants

In order to avoid a dauntingly long alphabetical list of shade-loving and shade-tolerant plants, it seems best to divide them into groups with similar needs or groups of similar habit. This also avoids the necessity of too large a number of symbols. We begin with shrubby calcifuges, those plants which insist on a lime-free soil. Thus readers who garden on lime have a splendid opportunity of skipping a whole chapter. Or nearly.

It has already been remarked more than once that successful gardening depends upon working with, not against, those natural factors of climate and soil with which each of us is blessed or cursed. (And it is psychologically sensible to presume the former.) This is nowhere more true than when trying to grow members of the *Ericaceae* on chalk . One of the most depressing garden sights I have ever had the misfortune to see was in a little valley in the South Downs where the sides, lining a little (artificial) stream, had been extravagantly planted with mature rhododendrons. Tons of peat had been imported, but still the plants were dying, chlorotically and in obvious pain. Not only did they resent the omnipresent lime in the soil and the soil water but also the lack of shade which, combined with the naturally free drainage, kept the plants in a state of near-drought.

This horticultural horror-story (sadly true) is equally ecologically unpleasant. We do not all go about consciously thinking of the positioned rightness of plants but any keen gardener develops an instinct of what looks innately right or wrong. And ericaceous woodlanders in an open limestone landscape is amongst the most blatant 'wrongs'. But if the 'I'm on lime' school is still with me there is a logical and possible way of being able to use some of the plants in this chapter.

To attempt to integrate the ecologically impossible into the natural landscape or informal parts of the garden must be

33

accepted as (to say the least) unwise. If they are to be grown, such plants must be brought to the obviously and acceptedly *made* areas close to the house or its associated buildings. The inevitable shady borders exist and can happily take that which would not grow — and look wrong if it did — in the open.

There is still the problem of providing the right growing medium but this is not difficult. Highly desirable are beds raised above the general soil level. Against a shady wall a yard-wide bed might be supported by a foot-high retaining wall in front. The existing soil is removed to a depth of a foot (300mm.) and the whole filled with a leafy lime-free medium.

This does not mean that limy water will not seep in or that roots of the bigger plants will not eventually extend into the limy substrate, but in courtyard shade, with its relatively high humidity, quite remarkable plants will flourish. I know one little courtyard, not far from the horrendous garden described above, where *Lapageria rosea* scrambles about 15ft (4·5m.) high camellias planted in 2ft (600mm.) of prepared border.

It must be emphasized, of course, that against any type of wall with a damp course the surface of the raised bed must either be below or the bed must stand free of the building, with both front and back walls of its own.

In such a situation — either the shady courtyard in a large site or a small town garden consisting of nothing else — the bigger, bushier rhododendrons will not be right but the sheltered position could be the home (if one is brave) for some of the thinner, tenderer *Maddenii* series rhododendrons. Similarly in small gardens the more delicate-looking x *Williamsii* camellias are to be preferred to the robust *Camellia japonica* cultivars. Certainly such gardens offer enormous scope to the keen plantsman, and a selection of plants follows. No apology is made for including plants whose tolerance of hard frost is low: woodland protection extends the range wonderfully.

In the lists most plants are given a height times width in feet, metres and millimetres. Flowering time is given but leaf effect is given equal importance in the text.

ADS = Accepts dry shade.

5 Shrubs for Shade: The Lime-haters

ACER. The maples or sycamores are usually more shade-providing than shade-loving trees, and the beautiful snake-barks (*A. davidii, A. grosseri* etc.) have already been recommended to that end. But the Japanese maples, especially in their delicately cut-leaved or golden forms are so apt to scorch in full sun, as does the brightest of the sycamores, *A. pseudoplatanus* 'Brilliantissimum', that they are best listed here.

japonicum *30 × 20ft (10 × 6m.) April*

While this, like the next species, can make a considerable, and very lovely tree — the sort of individual specimen that would be ideal in a small garden — it takes many years to get beyond the scale of a medium-sized shrub. Some lime is acceptable so long as the soil is deep and moist. Maples are not renowned as flowering plants but here the long-stalked clusters hang down from the bare branches to make quite a show. The leaves, however, are its chief glory.
—'**Aconitifolium**'. The fern-like leaves are deeply lobed and turn a good dark red in autumn. Deep shade will reduce, though not kill, autumn colour.
—'**Aureum**'. A very slow-growing form with leaves of a soft buttercup yellow.
—'**Vitifolium**'. The Vine-leaved Maple which produces such a magnificent show at Westonbirt Arboretum, near Stroud, Gloucestershire, every October and to which many people make considerable annual pilgrimages. Unlike many autumn-colourers which are constant in their colour this varies from plant to plant and even between branches on the same tree.

palmatum   *20 × 15ft (6 × 4·5m.)   April*

This is generally a smaller plant than the last. Having been cultivated for centuries in Japan before it was introduced to western Europe in the early nineteenth century, it exists in a large number of forms. Not for deep shade.

—**'Atropurpureum'** has soft red-purple leaves throughout the summer and is deservedly one of the most popular Japanese maples.

—**'Dissectum'** is the name given to a number of Japanese maples whose leaves have seven to ten lobes, each of which is subsequently divided to present a finely cut ferny effect. They are generally, even when mature, of medium shrub size, making a mound of elegant green or purple foliage. Some green forms, such as the well-known 'Ozakazuki' are renowned for their brilliant orange and scarlet autumn colour. Half shade is ideal here or the autumn effect becomes muted.

AMELANCHIER. These are the Snowy Mespilus of North American woodland. Species vary from low suckering shrubs such as *A. stolonifera* to small trees. In the spring the effect of clouds of white flowers, usually opening before the leaves, is charming but fleeting. Autumn colour is slightly more long-lasting. Light foliage encourages the herbaceous layer.

Nomenclature is highly confused with the name *A. canadensis* hovering over several distinct species. Yet as this is the name under which it is offered by the few nurseries that stock the genus it may as well remain here as an aggregate title. Further checks should be made in Hillier's Manual and the latest edition of *Bean's Trees and Shrubs* (1970): even here there is some disparity.

ANDROMEDA. A couple of little peat-bog plants of which the following is a rare British native.

polifolia   *1 × 1ft (300 × 300mm.)   June*

The pink bell flowers above blue-green leaves are very attractive, but it must be admitted that it does not make much of a show. Good in peat-block walls.

ARCTOSTAPHYLOS. A group of Ericaceous evergreens native mainly to the open coniferous forests of western Northern America especially in California and Oregon, where they are known as Manzanitas. They make distinctively architectural bushes with smooth mahogany bark rather like that of *Arbutus menziesii*. Difficult to obtain, one or two are worth trying in the dry shade of mature trees, so long as early care is assured.

canescens   *6 × 6ft (2 × 2m.)*

Stated by Bean as being one of the hardiest manzanitas and 'very decorative in spring when covered with its hoary young growth'.

pringlei   *8 × 10ft (2·5 × 3m.)*

Succeeds in London under holm oak and flowers well. The drooping spikes of pink urn-shaped flowers are attractive from March to May.

uva-ursi   *6in. − 5ft (150mm. × 1·5m.)*

This is the Bearberry of wide distribution in the Old and New worlds and makes excellent evergreen ground cover. Pink flowers in April and May followed by scarlet fruits. Again it is happy in dry shade under trees as well as accepting with gratitude more luxurious conditions. *A. nevadensis* is perhaps no more than a geographical variant.

CALLUNA.   *1 − 2 × 2ft (300 − 600 × 600mm.)*
July–November

This is the well-known ling or Scots heather which covers so many miles of open moorland in the north. In the south it is also seen, often taller, in typical associations on the 'Bagshot sands' with *Rhododendron ponticum* and silver birch. Here it accepts light shade and succeeds equally in dry and moist positions so long as the pH level is sufficiently low.

vulgaris is the only species but this has given rise to vast numbers of forms which have been collected both in the wild and from gardens. The typical September-flowering soft purple type can now be supplemented by others with colours ranging from white to pink and all shades of mauve, and flowering times from July to November. Many, too, are double and foliage can be golden, grey or bronze. Where possible, specialist nurseries or named collections should be visited. From this plethora amongst the best are:-
—**'Blazeaway'**. Flowers not spectacular but foliage turns red in winter, though less dramatically in shade than in the open.
—**'C. W. Nix'** has long feathery spikes of dark crimson flowers.
—**'Gold Haze'**. Here the white flowers are held against a background of bright golden foliage which is maintained throughout the year.
—**'H. E. Beale'**. This is, deservedly, one of the most popular heathers, with its long spikes of rose pink double flowers. 'Peter Sparkes' is similar; darker and later and good for succession.
—**'Serlei'** is perhaps the tallest Calluna, sometimes attaining 3ft in height, with masses of white flowers. It has produced forms with golden leaves ('Serlei Aurea') and dark red-purple flowers ('Serlei Rubra').
–**'Tib'** is amongst the first to come into bloom in July, with good double rosy-red spikes.

CAMELLIA.   *8 – 15 × 8 – 10ft (2·5 – 4·5 × 2·5 – 3m.)*
February–May

There is no doubt that for anyone with a bit of acid-soil shade a camellia or two is a 'must'. Few plants possess such shiny lustrous leaves as *C. japonica* and even if they never flowered they would be valuable evergreens and planted as such. But their truly exquisite flowers (it is too much to expect scent as well and only *C. sasanqua*, of those at all commonly grown, has a little), single, semi-double or formally fully-double in white through all shades of blush pink to darkest red, are unrivalled. Among plants we can grow in the open garden, their individual blossoms are finer than any shrub other than the rose.

'In the open garden' is a phrase consciously used here because the apparent exotic luxury of a camellia in full bloom seems to call for a range of heated greenhouses, or a fine Victorian conservatory at least. Indeed that is how they were once invariably treated (and certainly there are few more beautiful plants for an unheated house). It is, no doubt, for this reason that it took camellias a long time to break out from a 'caviare and oysters' image which prevented their more general use: this in no way detracts from their beauty but now offers (to egalitarian cheers) the horticultural equivalent of those delicious comestibles to all.

For as far as the plants are concerned they are unutterably frost-hardy. Not surprisingly, however, their great, almost fleshy, petals cannot remain unaffected, especially if touched by the early morning sun when frost is still in them. Thus, for such early-flowering plants — and 'Nobilissima', for example, rashly opens its first flowers soon after Christmas — some protection is desirable. This is best provided by careful positioning, avoiding an eastern exposure, in the shade of trees or west- or even north-facing walls if not fully exposed to winds. As has already been mentioned, shady courtyards provide admirable sites and certainly in London they flourish in the most unpromising situations.

A garden blessed with an area of woodland will obviously plant numbers of different camellia cultivars — and the range is truly daunting — while a small garden or town 'area' may only manage one or two. Choice is important because while all are good some are even better.

There are several points worthy of consideration which affect one's choice beyond the simple and relatively easy decision of colour. Even here one should consider the background — material of the wall behind, for instance; a fiery red flower is obviously not good against equally strong red brick. Habit varies between the vigorously upright scarlet 'Adolphe Audusson' and the broadly low-spreading pink 'Lady Clare', each magnificent examples of their type.

Another important consideration is whether, when the flowers are over (or sadly frosted) they drop whole or remain untidily and unsightly on the plant. If a shake brings them down all is well, but hand-picking on a large bush may well be unacceptable. In general the single forms are best at self-grooming.

Whereas the glossy-leaved *Camellia japonica* has been with us in increasing numbers of forms since the eighteenth century a second species of great significance to the garden is of much later introduction. Around 1917, George Forrest, the famous plant collector, sent seed of a new camellia from Yunnan in China. This was *C. saluenensis*, which was soon being grown at Caerhays Castle in Cornwall. It is a narrower-leaved, less shiny plant than the old 'japonicas', but lovely when covered with its single, soft pink, rather dog-rose-like flowers.

Crosses were soon being made between these two species, particularly by J. C. Williams at Caerhays Castle and by Colonel Stevenson Clarke at Borde Hill in Sussex. Botanically, as bi-specific hybrids, they bear the name of the first raiser, now followed of course by a cultivar name to distinguish each particular one. In general, *Williamsii* camellias can be recognized by their rather open habit, narrower leaves and mainly informal flowers, whether single or semi-double.

New crosses and selections are continually being made, especially in America and Australia: here are a few of the best, both old and new, to supplement those already mentioned.

Camellia japonica

—'Apple Blossom', a pale pink single to semi-double on a spreading bush.
—'Berenice Boddy'. One of the best Californian plants here. The growth is vigorous and upright with dark wavy leaves and

semi-double flowers which are mid pink in the centre and darken towards the outside.

—'**Contessa Lavinia Maggi**'. This old Italian cultivar has striped flowers as formal as the rosette on the side of its contemporary coachman's hat. Sometimes self-coloured flowers occur as well.

—'**Elegans**'. Another old plant of spreading form and big anemone-centred flowers of deep pink. It has been given every award in the book by the Royal Horticultural Society.

—'**Guilio Nuccio**'. A relatively new American variety with large semi-double flowers of a distinctive rose pink. A good strong grower.

—'**Jupiter**'. A splendid strong single scarlet with a great central boss of golden stamens.

—'**Magnoliaeflora**'. One of the most exquisite of flowers. Softest shell-pink of perfect form but inevitably susceptible to browning by heavy rain. 'Peach Blossom' is similar but darker in colour.

Camellia x williamsii

Although many of the recent hybrids exceed it in size and brightness the original Caerhays cross 'J. C. Williams' remains as beautiful as any. A rather diffuse shrub, it starts in March to open its elegant single flowers, soft clear translucent pink with a boss of yellow stamens. By April the bush is covered with them and stands as if in a pool, the reflection being the mass of still perfect blooms that have fallen to the ground. Further flowers continue to open till the end of May.

Other original *Williamsii* forms include 'St Ewe' with darker pink flowers which remain half-cupped, 'Mary Christian', a mid pink, and 'C. F. Coates'. This last is sometimes called the 'Fishtail Camellia' from the ends of its three-lobed leaves. 'Francis Hanger' and 'Coppelia Alba' are both white. For a sheltered corner close to the house, perhaps so that it gets a little extra warmth from a chimney-breast, nothing could be better than 'November Pink'. It really does start to flower then and keeps opening a few flowers whenever a mild period occurs. A few sprigs can always be found for the house and when the flowers fall another couple of days' pleasure can be gained by floating them in a bowl as a table centre.

Further *Williamsii* camellias which must be mentioned include:

'Debbie'. A strong upright grower but with almost weeping side-branches bowed down with rose pink paeony-like flowers.

'Donation'. A famous plant making a tall narrow bush and annually covered with big semi-double rather loose flowers. These are a clear pink with darker veins. Without doubt this is amongst the easiest camellias to satisfy, succeeding in cold gardens way up in Scotland.

'Elsie Jury'. Clear soft pink flowers that have been described as resembling a formal Victorian presentation posy: two outside rows of petals supporting a rosette of waved petalodes and stamens. All this on a strong hardy bush.

Camellia reticulata

This huge plant is not for cold gardens and unsheltered places though some forms of the single wild type, not unlike a big 'Williamsii' but having the typical netted leaves of its name, are much hardier than was first thought. *Camellia reticulata* was first known in 1820 in Europe in a lovely semi-double form (now called 'Captain Rawes' after its introducer, a member of the East India Company). It is still one of the most sumptuous shrubs that can be grown outside in this country and justifies every care on a high wall or bit of sheltered woodland: foliage and habit can be a bit coarse, however.

This and other early introductions came from gardens in the (Chinese) treaty ports. It was only quite recently that it became known that many other varieties of *C. reticulata* were to be found in the gardens of cities deep in the interior of China, in the province of Yunnan'.[1]

[1]Bean: *Trees and Shrubs Hardy in the British Isles, 1970.*

Since their arrival in the 1950s breeders, particularly in America, have brought reticulata blood into many new hybrids with *C. japonica* and C. × *williamsii*. While varieties of these latter species are always likely to be the staple fare of most of our gardens there is no doubt that hardier reticulatas are on their way. So far the best are:

—'**Mary Williams**', a Caerhays selection with large single deep-rose flowers.

—'**Francie L**'. Large semi-double flowers of clear rose red; the waved petals surround a splendid boss of yellow stamens.

—'**Salutation**'. This lovely plant was raised at Borde Hill, between *C. reticulata* and *C. saluenensis*. The informal semi-double flowers are of softest pink. Good in woodland, with a better habit than most.

Of other camellia species so far undescribed here *C. sasanqua* needs too much sun to ripen its wood to justify inclusion with shade-lovers, *C. granthamiana* is ravishing but really a greenhouse plant while *C. cuspidata* is, by comparison with its relations, frankly undistinguished. However, its cross with *C. saluenensis*, known as 'Cornish Snow' — especially in the clone 'Michael' — does have considerable charm. Leaves are small on a big twiggy bush which covers itself with further small (for a camellia) white flowers from February onwards.

CLETHRA. The sweet-pepper bushes are useful late-flowering mainly deciduous shrubs with spikes of pleasantly scented flowers. The finest species are unfortunately the most frost tender but might be tried by the brave.

alnifolia. *8 × 6ft (2·5 × 2m.)   August*

The best form of this North American species is known as 'Paniculata' with fine white spikes. It enjoys a moist spot in open woodland. 'Rosea' is pink in bud and the two forms look well together.

arborea   *20 × 15ft (6 × 4·5m.)   July*

This is one of the many lovely plants native to that 'Island of Flowers', Madeira. As such it is on the borderline of hardiness with a few of us and way beyond it for most, but as splendid plants exist in some of the great gardens of south west England, Ireland and west Scotland, suitable sites might be found in places of lesser pretension. Every care is justified for this remarkable evergreen.

delavayi   *20 − 30 × 20ft (6 − 10 × 6m.)   July*

From Yunnan, this is only marginally inferior, with its lily-of-the-valley-like spikes, to the previous species. The size sounds daunting but it flowers when relatively young and is noticeably hardier, but still a plant for a west wall or preferably woodland in all but the warmest gardens.

Other Clethras from the Orient include *C. barbidensis, C. fargesii* and *C. monostachya*. All are worth trying if only they can be obtained.

CORNUS. This big genus will have to be listed here as well as in the next section of lime-tolerant shrubs. Fortunately it divides easily from a visual point of view as well as cultivationally. Here, for organic soils (a little liminess deep down is accepted) are the lovely flowering dogwoods, whose button-like clusters of tiny flowers are surrounded by big petal-like bracts, the whole appearing like one large open flower.

In the woodlands of eastern North America from Georgia north to the Niagara peninsula of Ontario the dogwoods light up the woods with their snowy flowers before the leaf canopy above unfolds. Other, somewhat similar, species come from the Orient and western North America.

capitata   *20 − 40 × 20 − 30ft (6 − 12 × 6 − 9m.)   June*

This marvellous plant, introduced from the eastern Himalayas in 1825, is sadly on the borderline of hardiness but in some Cornish woodland gardens it sows itself by the hundred. The 'flowers' are creamy yellow and are often succeeded by straw-berry-like fruit in sufficient quality to make a second display in autumn.

florida This is the eastern American dogwood and, adapted to a severe continental climate, is happier away from the moister western side. In some Bournemouth gardens, for example, it has done well, as does the exquisite pink form. Susceptible to spring frosts, it needs, like camellias, protection from the eastern sun. A few named cultivars from America are becoming available here, such as 'Apple Blossom' and 'White Cloud', which describe themselves and 'Cherokee Chief', a deep rose red. Sheltered woodland in dry East Anglia might offer a suitable home.

kousa   *15 − 20 × 10ft (4·5 − 6 × 3m.)   June–July*

This lovely oriental holds its 'flowers' erect on slender stalks and they line the nearly horizontal branches like whirling-skirted dancers on a vast stage. It will take some lime in the soil so long as depth and moisture are adequate: sun also is acceptable but a glade in open woodland is to be preferred.

The variety *chinensis* is a more robust form but otherwise similar. Foliage develops purplish tints before the last bracts fall.

nuttallii   *20 − 30 × 15 − 20ft (6 − 10 × 4·5 − 6m.)   May*

The Pacific Dogwood is of a tree stature, attaining 100 feet/ 30m. in the forests of Oregon and British Columbia. Here it is smaller and, it often seems, not long-lived. Yet, as it flowers at an early age it is well worth growing. Each 'flower' has usually six large bracts, which are white with a pink flush. Autumn colour is often good and so gives an end-of-year bonus.

CORYLOPSIS. Although related to Hamamelis and Parottia this lovely genus much more resembles, as its name suggests, the hazels or Corylus. But the resemblance is superficial in that the soft yellow spikes though hanging down like hazel's lamb's tails, are complete insect-pollinated flowers, not the anemophilous male catkins they seem. The delicate yet penetrating scent of cowslips too will obviously attract, something which plants that depend upon the wind do not need. The half-dozen or so species all flower before the leaves and enjoy overhead woodland protection or a western half-shaded aspect in cold gardens: they can be disappointing in areas subject to late spring frosts, losing not only flowers but young leaves as well. No plant takes that for long. As an alternative to the ubiquitous forsythia, with its often hard-yellow flowers and inelegant shape, corylopsis should be recommended. While preferring leafy, woodland soils only *C. pauciflora* is actually antipathetic to lime.

glabrescens   *15 × 15ft (4·5 × 4·5m.)   March–April*

This plant from Japan and other orientals including *platypetala* (W. China), *sinensis*, of which the preceding may be a variety, *veitchiana* (W. China) and *spicata* (Japan) are all fine spreading shrubs and somewhat similar to each other.

pauciflora   *4 − 6 × 5ft (1·2 − 2 × 1·5m.)   March*

As this lovely little shrub has the largest flowers (though fewer to a spike) of any other species we grow it illustrates to perfection the occasional, and heartening, fallibility of botanical nomenclature. Enjoys moist shade and associates beautifully with other choice woodland plants. Young leaves are pink throughout summer.

willmottiae   *12 × 8ft (4 × 2·5m.)*

Distinctive with its purplish opening leaves, for which virtue a named clone 'Spring Purple' has been selected.

CRINODENDRON hookeranum   *10 − 20 × 10 − 15ft (3 − 6 × 3 − 4·5m.)   May–June*

Coming from Chilean forests, this is a plant for our milder, moister gardens yet such is its beauty that anyone with a shady, sheltered wall will try it. It has, however, the foolish habit of putting out its flower buds in September where they hang to survive the winter — or not — and to depress the owner in every cold snap. Nonetheless success is worth waiting for, when they swell and develop into glowing rose pink lanterns in their background of dark green leaves. If it can be placed to get a flash of low, late evening sun the flower colour brightens to scarlet. It is sometimes still offered under its old synonym *Tricuspidaria lanceolata*.

DABOECIA cantabrica   *2 × 2ft (600 × 600mm.)*
June–October

This is the charming Connemara heath, growing wild in western Ireland and down into Spain. The individual flowers, in bright rose purple, white or pink, are the biggest of any hardy heather and make a fine long-lasting display. While happily taking full sun it is also content with the light shade of, for example, silver birch in an association with other heather garden plants.

DESFONTAINEA spinosa   *10 × 10ft (3 × 3m.)*
July–October

Another Chilean plant enjoying similar conditions to Crino-dendron but is, in general, less frost-sensitive. Nonetheless it does best away from the more continental climate of say, East Anglia. In south west Scotland it is an outstanding success, suddenly producing from what for all the world appeared a perfectly ordinary holly, long waxy tubes of yellow and scarlet. It flowers well even on very small plants and very slowly attains its ultimate size. Perhaps it could be tried more: for years I grew it as a tub plant in a shady courtyard in maritime Hampshire and when it got too big it went to a woodland glade in Oxfordshire without, apparently, looking back.

DISANTHUS cercidifolius   *10 × 10ft (3 × 3m.)*

Probably unobtainable, this pleasant Japanese woodlander has insignificant purplish flowers rather like those of Hamamelis, to which it is related. But the Judas-tree-like leaves colour magnificently beginning in August — the whole resembles rather a small cercidiphyllum, which must be sufficient recommendation for anything.

DISTYLIUM racemosum   *10 × 8ft (3 × 2·5m.)*

Another witch-hazel relative, but evergreen this time. Again flowers are not spectacular. Lacking petals, the stamens are responsible for the reddish colouring. But it is a distinctive plant with its fan-like branching and succeeds even in the shade of sycamores.

DRIMYS winteri   *10 – 30 × 10 – 20ft (3 – 10 × 3 – 6m.)*

This is now placed in its own family of *Winteraceae*, not far removed botanically from the magnolias. Whereas it can make a vast plant in favoured gardens — and given the space — it is suitable for shady walls (west-facing for preference) in at least half the country or in woodland. Potential growers need not be daunted by the top figures given. While it reaches tree size in warm woodland, it can easily be kept in bounds on an eight-foot wall. The long evergreen aromatic leaves have fine milk-white undersides which flash in the wind. Having settled down to flower it does so for several months from March — loose heads of ivory white.

andina is a very dwarf variety collected in its Andean home at about 4000 feet. This starts to flower when a couple of feet high and takes years to double it. Drimys accept lime in a deep moist soil, but are probably happier without it.

EMBOTHRIUM   *15 – 20 × 10ft (4·5 – 6 × 3m.)*

Another Chilean and as remarkable as any of its geographical fellows. In the best and hardiest forms such as that sometimes called 'Norquinco Valley' (*E. coccineum lanceolatum*) the flower clusters touch each other on the branches so that the whole plant appears a pillar of vermilion. 'Chilean Fire-bush' is a most satisfactory name.

It enjoys the moist, leafy sort of open woodland but more than half shade inhibits flowering. One point should not be forgotten: its truly extraordinary colour does not mix happily with rhododendron reds, especially those with any hint of blue in them.

Embothriums must be planted young from pots because they cannot stand root disturbance; even then it must be admitted plants can pop off with no warning. But such is the lure that one is bound to try again.

EMPETRUM nigrum   *1 × 5ft (300mm. × 1·5m.)*

This is our native crowberry, a moorland plant, which associates well with other low ericaceous things and makes good ground cover in half shade.

ENKIANTHUS. This genus, though never common, can be one of the pleasures of light woodland. Growth is open and tiered and the small bell-shaped flowers hang down like currants. All species have in addition marvellous autumn colour, which, it has been suggested, is unsurpassed by any other genus. Half-shade only.

campanulatus   *8 − 10 × 6ft (2·5 − 3 × 2m.)   May*

Perhaps the easiest to please with dark yellow to bronze veined flowers covering the plant in good years.

cernuus rubens   *6 − 8 × 6ft (2 − 2·5 × 2m.)   May*

This is the brightest in flower, especially if the bells can be seen with the light behind them, when they appear to have switched on their own internal illumination.

Other species include *chinensis*, yellow with red veining, and *perulatus*, a lovely white. It is hoped they will remain available from specialist nurserymen.

ERICA. The heathers are not plants for deep shade but they do enjoy the half-shade of thin woodland right up to the boles of trees, where, if looked after in the first year or two, they seem able to withstand tree-induced drought remarkably well. Colour can be obtained from the genus in every month of the year as well as plants of surprising diversity of size from large shrubs to dwarf ground-coverers. It is perhaps best to group them here according to type.

Tree Heaths. Spring-flowering.

ERICA arborea alpina   *10 × 8ft (3 × 2·5m.)   March–April*

While the true species is a lovely plant, attaining up to 20 feet or so it is less reliably hardy than this form, which was originally collected in 1892 in the mountains of Spain. 'Alpina' takes some years to settle down to flower well but this is of little importance because of its value as a foliage plant. It makes lovely heaps of fresh ferny green against which other, brighter-flowered, calcifuges are well sited. It is also particularly beautiful when placed with silver birches.

australis   *6 × 8ft (2 × 2·5m.)   April–June*

This is the brightest of the tree heathers (though not one of the hardiest) with rose-purple flowers which should be used carefully within sight of scarlet rhododendrons or the young growth of *Pieris forrestii*. 'Mr Robert' is a fine white form: both this and the type can be gawky plants and should be pruned back after flowering.

erigena   *4 × 6ft (1·2 × 2m).   March–May*

This name for the excellent and easy plant — the best of the true heaths for general planting — has now replaced the epithet '*mediterranea*'. Here is an occasion to welcome a name-change because the plant's distribution, right down the west side of Europe, from Co. Mayo to Spain, does not include any Mediterranean littoral; it is nice to be *helped* not hindered by a new name. It is one of the few heaths that will accept a little lime in the soil but it is a mistake to think it likes it. Several good forms exist: 'Superba' is pink and 6 feet high, 'W. T. Rackliff' a tight-growing white-flowered type while 'Brightness' and 'Coccinea' are both small with flower colour living up to their names.

lusitanica *6 − 10 × 6ft (2 − 3 × 2m.)   February–April*

The tall narrow spikes of the Portuguese heather make it a striking plant for several months in late winter and early spring. The myriad buds are noticeably pink before they open to a clearer white than that of *E. arborea*. Like the other big tree-heaths, it is not for the coldest gardens.

Dwarf Heaths. Winter- and spring-flowering.

herbacea *1 − 2 × 2ft (300 − 600 × 600mm.)*
December–April

The change of name from *E. carnea* will probably be ignored for sometime to come but what is more important is to reaffirm that there is no more valuable winter/early spring-flowering plant for providing swathes of colour in sun or the half-shade of woodland. There are a couple of dozen named forms, varying in colour, size and time of flowering. All are good and a visit to any extensive heather garden will show up the best, amongst which are:–
—'King George' ('Winter Beauty'), bright rose pink,
—'Springwood Pink' is paler, and 'Springwood White', the best white. Both 'Springwoods' have distinctive trailing growth which rapidly colonizes bare ground. 'Vivellii' is a tighter plant, with deep carmine-red flowers set off against the winter bronzed foliage.

x **darleyensis** *3 × 2ft (1m. × 600mm.)   November–April*

Hybrids between *E. herbacea* and *E. erigena*, which combine admirably the attributes of both species. 'Darley Dale' is the original type, which appeared by chance about 1890 with pale pink flowers in long spikes, excellent for cutting. 'George Rendall' is darker pink and 'Silberschmelze' the best white.

    With both the above species care must be taken with their calcifuge associates: scarlet camellias or early rhododendrons are best kept with the grey-whites of tree heaths or later-flowering things. The softer pinks, however, of most 'Williamsii' camellias and many dwarf rhododendrons will associate happily.

Summer Heaths.

By July, although there are still some lovely things to come there is apt to be the feeling that the woodland garden has passed its prime and that we can now only look to the herbaceous border, the bedding and the roses. Fortunately this is not true, even for those gardening on thin acid soils, often unkind to such plants. So, though not for deep shade, those ericas (all forms of native plants) which flower from late June to November are very useful indeed and associate naturally with Calluna and Daboecia.

ciliaris *1 × 1½ft (300 – 460mm.)   July–October*

This is the Dorset Heath, which is rather like a larger-flowered version of 'Bell Heather'. 'Maweana' (rosy red) and 'Stoborough' (white) are both reliable and available.

cinerea *1 × 1½ft (300 – 450mm.)   June–September*

This is our common 'Bell Heather' which covers miles of moorland from Cornwall to North Scotland. Pink, red, purple and white forms are available as are others with interesting foliage effects. 'Golden Drop' is well described for summer but with colder weather its leaves turn red.

tetralix   *1 × 1½ft (300 × 450mm.)   June–October*

The grey to nearly silver foliage of the best forms of the 'Cross-leaved Heath' makes a good foil to the hotter colours of 'Bell Heather'. 'Alba Mollis' and 'Con Underwood' are respectively white and crimson.

vagans   *1 – 2 × 2 – 4ft (300 × 600 × 600mm. – 1·2m.) July–October*

Again, for glades in open woodland or where a couple of trees meet the lawn, this is an admirable plant for long late-summer interest. It carries long spikes of flowers which may be deep pink ('Mrs D. F. Maxwell'), softer rosy pink ('St Keverne') or white ('Lyonesse').

The less sun heathers get the less tight is their growth, especially if the garden soil is richer, as is likely, than that of their moorland homes. A clipping over in spring before the new season's growth begins is wise, perhaps every other year. If those cut are not all in the same area an over-manicured effect will be avoided. This is desirable; in spite of so many ericas having cultivars of garden or natural origins and the fact that there are even bi-specific hybrids, there is still the feeling in most cases that one is growing wild plants. This ambience, however illusory, of moorland and rough places should not be carelessly discarded.

EUCRYPHIA. A group of often large and generally evergreen shrubs from the southern hemisphere. Such distribution inevitably reduces their use in cold gardens yet a couple are amongst the most beautiful plants we can grow and relish the shade of open woodland and the protection it gives. Their scented white flowers, varying in size from 1 to 3 inches (25 – 80mm.) across, resemble snowy St John's worts with their great central boss of stamens. All flower in late summer and early autumn: lacecap hydrangeas look particularly well clustering round the foot of large specimens and combine to make an eye-stopping August/ September picture.

cordifolia. Eventually a tall narrow tree up to 70 feet (21m.) in height and suitable only for big gardens in the west, moisture and lack of searing frost being appreciated. But to its hybrid with *E. glutinosa* it has passed on a surprising tolerance to lime which is shared by none other of the genus. This is the invaluable:-

x nymansensis.   *30 – 40 × 8ft (10 – 13 × 2·5m.)*
August–September

There can be few more lovely trees when the narrow evergreen spire becomes white with flower and few more suitable plants of its height for small gardens. Deep shade is likely to reduce flowering but in a semi-shaded town garden, as well as for grander country woodland edge, it could be used as a focal point for the whole design.

glutinosa   *10 – 15 × 10ft (3 – 4·5 × 3m.)   July–August*

This is the other parent of x *nymanensis*, which provides its hardiness and again, in flower, is a plant of outstanding beauty. This is compounded by the brilliant autumn colour of its deciduous leaves. It is highly calcifuge and insists upon a peaty or leafy soil. Shade at the root seems essential for good growth, especially when young. It is an ideal associate in a mainly rhododendron garden to extend season and interest.

lucida   *15 – 20 × 6 – 8ft (4·5 – 6 × 2 – 2·5m.)   June–July*

Though not for cold gardens, this Tasmanian species is relatively hardy, enjoying woodland or west-wall conditions and making a huge tree in Cornwall. The flowers are noticeably more pendulous and the stamens bright pink when the cup of petals is newly opened.

x intermedia   *20 × 10ft (6 × 3m.)*

This cross between the two previous species seems to combine the garden-worthy properties of both, being hardier (for a Eucryphia, that is), fast-growing and flowering at an early age. It is geographically interesting as combining Chilean and Tasmanian genes.

In addition to a further couple of species there are also other hybrids and named clones of those already mentioned; while it must be accepted that they are, with the exception of x *nymansensis*, in some doubt as to frost-tolerance, anyone with a suitable bit of woodland is bound to try them.

FOTHERGILLA. From eastern North America these witch-hazel relations enjoy similar conditions to azaleas and Enkianthus. Open woodland or association with taller shrubs is ideal, though too much shade reduces the brightness of autumn colour.

major   *6 × 6ft (2 × 2m.)   April–May*

The flower spikes, appearing before the leaves are fully developed, are like creamy green bottle brushes, composed of stamens pink on the stalk. *F. monticola* is rather similar, *F. gardenii* stays small, around 3 − 4ft (1 − 1·2m.).

GAULTHERIA. A big Ericaceous genus of interesting plants varying from the little ground-coverers to medium-sized shrubs. All enjoy at least some shade in leafy soil. Amongst the best are:–

forrestii   *5 × 5ft (1·5 × 1·5m.)   April–May*

White, urn-shaped fragrant flowers make a fine display against the dark, luxuriant foliage. In a good year a second show of blue berries is noteworthy.

procumbens *6in. × 3ft (150mm. × 1m.)   April–May*

The North American Checkerberry, making mats of dark foliage. The small white flowers are followed by scarlet fruits in autumn. Ideal ground cover for a shady bank.

shallon ADS   *2 – 4 × 3ft (600mm. – 1·2 × 1m.)   May*

If it were rare or difficult to grow we should hail this as the finest of the genus. But fortunately it is neither, accepting even ever-green-oak shade right against the bole. Depending on conditions, it will vary in vigour considerably but always with dark evergreen foliage and upstanding spikes of pinkish flowers on pinker stalks. Edible (just) purple berries follow.

A cross between this and *Pernettya mucronata* is called x *Gaulnettya wisleyensis*, indicating its place of origin. Interesting, with sufficient white bells to make a spring show and dark red berries, but not really as striking as either parent. Closely related, too, are the species of *Lyonia* offering similar urn-shaped pinkish or white flowers for similar positions.

HALESIA. Of a size to be shade-producing the snowdrop tree in its North American home shares woodlands with dogwoods and other plants to make a high shrub layer. Here the profusion of flower is seen admirably from below: the effect of a well-grown plant is physically fleeting but memorable.

carolina   *10 – 20 × 15ft (3 – 6 × 4·5m.)   May*

Covers itself with flowers — although the season is short — when most of the cherries have gone over. *H. monticola* is similar but much bigger.

HAMAMELIS. Without doubt the witch-hazels are the finest of winter-flowering shrubs. While accepting both lime, in deep soil, and full sun, they are best given some summer shade in a cool leafy soil. Typical flowers are made up of long spidery petals which are able to withstand considerable frost.

japonica   *10 × 15ft (3 × 4·5m.)   January–February*

Yellow flowers in profusion on a striking tiered bush. The distinctive shape makes an admirable focal point.

mollis   *10 × 10ft (3 × 3m.)   December–February*

Strongly scented and bigger individual flowers ('Pallida' is even bigger) making a fine show for many weeks in the depths of winter. The summer foliage is soft and downy, hazel-like, and turns a good clear autumn yellow. Hybrids between these two species are offered under several clonal names. They incorporate virtues from both parents, lacking only the perfume of *mollis*. Most distinctive are the dark-flowered forms such as the lovely 'Jelena', a fine coppery-orange.

KALMIA. Distinctive calcifuges from North America needing conditions similar to those for azaleas. Growing naturally in semi-bog areas they are most intolerant of drought, and shade, it must be admitted, is only an alternative to copious moisture.

angustifolia   *3 × 2ft (1m. × 600mm.)   June*

Dark rose flowers in heads above the narrow evergreen leaves. A useful front-line shrub.

latifolia   *6 − 8 × 5 − 6ft (2 − 2·5 × 1·5 − 2m.)   June*

The distinctive Calico Bush with its quaintly crimped flowers. When doing well it is amongst the brightest sights the June garden can provide.

polifolia   *2 × 2ft (600 × 600mm.)   June*

Good pink flowers and foliage with brilliant glaucous reverse.

LEDUM. A small group of low-growing Kalmia relations and needing similar conditions of moist acid soil and accepting part shade.

groenlandicum *2 × 2ft (600 × 600mm.)   April–June*

Typical of the genus with heads of white flowers for quite a long period in spring above netted evergreen leaves.

LEUCOTHÖE. More ericoids of considerable value under trees in acid soils. They are used much more in the United States, from where the following species, amongst others, comes.

fontanesiana (catesbei) *6 × 6ft (2 × 2m.)   May*

Lovely arching wands carry long, narrow leaves and spikes of white pieris-shaped flowers in their axils. Although evergreen the foliage takes on purplish tints in less than half-shade. While not as accommodating as *Gaultheria shallon*, this fine plant will accept surprisingly dry positions if started off well.

LOMATIA. Belonging to the same family, the *Proteaceae*, as Embothrium, this is a group of large shrubs from the southern hemisphere. All have unusual evergreen leaves, narrow, leathery and long-fingered, sometimes attractively backed with a suede-like indumentum. While being seen at their best in west of England woodland they offer an interesting challenge for shady walls (against, not trained) up country.

ferruginea *15 − 30 × 10ft (4·5 − 10 × 3m.)   June–July*

The orange and scarlet flowers are in fact of less import than the general foliage pattern. Like evergreen ferns on a big bush they emerge coated with brownish-crimson fur. This plant grows naturally with *Eucryphia cordifolia* on Chiloe Island, Chile. Even if occasional hard frosts keep it small it is well worth a place.

myracoides *8 × 8ft (2·5 × 2·5m.)   July*

Hooked white flowers, heavily fragrant, are carried well enough to make a show; but here again it is the long narrow-toothed leaves which are particularly distinctive. From south-east Australia, this plant has proved surprisingly hardy in the south of England.

MAGNOLIA. It might be better in some ways to devote a whole section to this marvellous genus not only because of its range of types, tree or shrub, evergreen or deciduous, but because it bridges the cultivational divide of calcifuge or calcicole and hence is not restricted to this particular section. Generally magnolias do not *need* shade yet like camellias their early flowers are wisely protected from the early morning sun and as with many rhododendrons, woodland association, where this can be contrived, gives a far more satisfying effect. In the context of this list they fall into three main groups.

1 Asiatic tree magnolias

Eventually making full forest-tree size and flowering foolishly early in the year, it may seem positively perverse to list these at all. But if planting only a dozen is encouraged thereby the effort will not have been wasted. They are, it must be admitted, slow to come into flower — twenty years from seed is usual with *M. campbellii* — but bought-in plants, especially if vegetatively propagated, reduce this period: in any case large flowers on a small plant would look silly. Members of this group are seen best, not least because they have been there the longest, in great Cornish gardens such as Caerhays Castle; but later plantings at Windsor, Kew and elsewhere should encourage us further.

campbellii (+ subspecies and cultivars) *Tree March*

The group is centred round this great Himalayan. Huge flowers, not much less than a foot across, are like glowing pink water-lilies carried on bare branches. A plant in full flower is an extraordinary sight and worth travelling far to see. The feast is a maddeningly movable one, however, and may well be over or completely unready if plans are made too soon. A good method is to base the pilgrimage upon the famous tree in the National Trust garden (hence often open) of Sharpitor in Salcombe, South Devon. Local knowledge must be sought by telephone: is it coming out? do the nights appear relatively frost-free? Then off: any of half a dozen or more weekends from late February to mid April are possible. Such a trip will ensure, like Jenner's early inoculating experiments with cow-pox, that the bug is well and truly caught.

mollicomata. A hardier subspecies from Yunnan and Tibet, this flowers earlier in life and on a narrower tree, more suitable for smaller spaces. It could well be used as the one specimen tree in a sheltered and half-shady town garden. Flowers are dark pink towards purple in some forms.

Crosses between this and *campbellii* itself offer hybrid vigour and desirable attributes from both parents. They include 'Charles Raffill', 'Kew's Surprise' and 'Wakehurst'.

There are other big-flowered tree magnolias for large gardens such as *dawsoniana, sprengeri* and *sargentiana robusta*. Of the latter a doyen of magnolia specialists, that great Cornish gardener the late G. H. Johnstone, made a diary entry dated 13.4.31: 'I was privileged today to see *Magnolia sargentiana robusta* flowering at Caerhays for the first time in this country. I do not hesitate to say that it is the most beautiful of all the magnolias I have yet seen in flower. The flowers, formed with twelve sepals, are semi-pendulous at the ends of the spreading branches, and in size appear to be about 8–12 inches in diameter, in colour pale rose-purple shading to pale pink at the tips. Looking up into the blooms, they appeared like opening parachutes of coloured paper, their beauty accentuated by black scales of unopened or partly opened buds.' All of these plants may start life in the shelter of woodland; soon their size makes them a part of it.

2 Smaller magnolias

For smaller gardens there are smaller magnolias. Although fine specimens are seen in full sun, to avoid petal-bleach as well as giving protection from wind and frost, a bit of shade makes all the difference.

kobus might be described as a small-flowered tree magnolia which will eventually attain 30 feet (10m.) or so, covered in March and April when mature with white flowers.

stellata is often considered to be a tight shrubby variant of the above species. It seldom exceeds 10 feet in height and indeed takes decades to approach it. For this reason it is frequently recommended as *the* magnolia for small gardens. Certainly the size is right but it seems to need the moral support and protection of other plants around it: not a plant for isolation and its low flowers are very susceptible to frost.

x **loebneri** combines the virtues of the two previous species in a miraculous way. The early floriferousness of the otherwise rather costive *stellata* is combined with the free open growth and lime tolerance of *kobus*. The type is white while 'Leonard Messel' is a lovely pink. Other selections are sometimes available. Similar in habit is the delicate *M. salicifolia* with narrow leaves, white flowers and lemon-scented bark. This could well be used more.

There is no doubt that the most popular of the genus is x *soulangeana* with its vertically-held vase-shaped flowers varying in colour from white to deep purple pink. Though not liking shallow chalky soils it accepts clays with relative equanimity. Eventually making a huge wide-spreading shrub, it flowers when very young — albeit the blooms ridiculously dwarf the branches they sit on. Many clones have been named since M. Soulange-Bodin's first cross made in the nineteenth century. 'Alexandrina' (white), 'Lennei' (cream and mulberry shaded) and 'Rustica Rubra' (rosy red) are but three: it is best to visit a collection in flower before deciding on the only one one has room for. Both the parents, *denudata* and *liliiflora* are well worth planting if space permits, the former a perfect white.

3 Late-flowering magnolias

A final group of magnolias are late spring- to early summer-flowering plants, making tall sparse shrubs and particularly lovely pendulous flowers of transluscent white, each with a purple or crimson 'eye' of stamens. *Wilsonii* and *sinensis* are rather similar species (the latter is marginally more striking) and a putative hybrid between the two is x *highdownensis*. All plantsmen immediately recognize such an epithet as being synonymous with chalk tolerance, and so it is here. The display in June is spectacular but short. Extending the season from May to August, a few flowers opening every day, is the exquisite *sieboldii*, with a perfume evocative of gardenias washed down in lemon juice. All members of this group appreciate some shade and help to continue the interest in a garden that is apt to concentrate heavily upon earlier-flowering rhododendrons and azaleas.

A last thought: though it is seldom seen, anyone with a bit of moist, even boggy woodland should plant *Magnolia virginiana*. This is the Swamp Bay. The narrow leaves — a few stay on all winter — are brilliant white underneath and flash in the wind like Drimys. The flowers are the size, shape and colour of pheasants' eggs with an utterly unique and delicious scent — a perfect table-centre for a summer evening.

MENZIESIA. Another little group of Ericaceous plants of which one, particularly, is useful to extend the range of interest.

ciliicalyx *3 × 2ft (1m. × 600mm.) May*

Softly downy deciduous leaves and clusters of urn-shaped flowers, cream, pale pink or near purple. Other, named, forms are occasionally offered and are well worth obtaining.

MITCHELLA repens is the Partridge Berry of eastern North America. On a small scale it makes good evergreen ground cover under shrubs, with little shiny paired leaves and pinkish flowers in the axils in June. Bead-sized scarlet fruits follow.

MITRARIA coccinea. From the far south of the Americas comes another ground-hugger. In the wild, in the wet southern forests, it often behaves epiphytically. 'Often', says Good-speed[1] 'we were aware of its presence overhead only by fallen petals at the foot of the tree which it had climbed'.

Here, in the moist shade of other shrubs it makes a hummock of low growth and hangs out its mitre-shaped flowers, near vermilion in colour. Not for cold gardens.

MYRICA. Interesting associates for ericas but in no more than half shade. Plants with aromatic leaves, to crush as one passes, are always a delight.

cerifera *6 × 6ft (2 × 2m.) May*

The Wax Myrtle of south eastern North America makes little effect in flower but the fruits are interesting in that their waxy covering has been used from colonial times to make deliciously fragrant candles and soaps.

gale *3 × 3ft (1 × 1m.) April*

Our native 'Bog Myrtle' bears tiny flowers in catkin-like heads (the sexes on separate plants). It will accept the most acid and boggy situations where little else woody will grow.

OXYDENDRUM arboreum. *10 − 15 × 8ft (3 − 4·5 × 2·5m.) July–August*

A lovely late-flowering shrub — occasionally of small tree size, to extend interest in the Rhododendron garden. Where not too shaded the leaves colour dramatically before falling. It is one of

[1]*Plant Hunters in the Andes.*

the few plants that have won Royal Horticultural Society's Awards of Merit both for flower (1957) and autumn foliage colour (1951).

PERNETTYA mucronata. *2 − 3 × 3ft (600mm. − 1m. × 1m.)   May*

This splendid suckering South American evergreen is happy in full sun, but in the garden with heathery associates it succeeds equally well in the light shade of silver birches. In the wild it grows right down to the Straits of Magellan, the dread Cape Horn of sailing ships, so is remarkably hardy. In May and June its prickly thickets are white with flower but its real claim to our attention comes in autumn when covered with marble-sized berries which last for months.

A whole range of colour forms exists, with suitably evocative names: 'Cherry Ripe', 'Lilacina', 'Mulberry Wine', 'White Pearl' are but four. 'Bell's Seedling', a good dark red, is also valuable as being definitely hermaphrodite but it is always wise to plant Pernettyas in groups to ensure pollination.

PHILESIA magellanica. *2 × 2ft (600 × 600mm.)*
July–September

A compatriot of Pernettya but vastly different. A close relation of the climbing Lapageria (qv) and, more distantly, the lilies, this makes a low clump of suckering wiry stems. Its narrow evergreen leaves are joined in summer by waxy tubes like crimson forms of *Rhododendron cinnabarinum*.

Philesia needs a moist peaty soil, shade and shelter in a not-cold spot. As so often with these South American forest plants it is seen best with us (where it is seen at all) in western gardens, especially in Scotland.

PIERIS. A gem of a genus for shade and acid soils with generally white urn-shaped flowers in copious drooping panicles, like bunches of Lily of the Valley worn as a corsage. Young growth is often brilliantly coloured.

floribunda   *5 × 5ft (1·5 × 1·5m.)   March–April*

A North American and the first Pieris to be brought into cultivation. It is very hardy, with erect spikes of flowers.

forrestii   *8 × 10ft (2·5 × 3m.)   April*

This is now usually accorded subspecific status of *P. formosa*. Oblivious of botanical nicety it is one of the most striking plants our woodland gardens can grow and huge panicles of flowers, hardly smaller than bunches of grapes, are succeeded by poinsettia-like shuttlecocks of brilliant red leaves which gradually become green.

There are several selected forms of which 'Jermyns' and 'Wakehurst' are two of the best. While *Pieris forrestii* is reasonably hardy in its mature growth it must be remembered that the young growth is very susceptible to May frosts: overhead protection and from the east is desirable. There are few sorrier sights than yesterday's scarlet growths browned overnight; and it does of course weaken the plant.

japonica   *6 × 5ft (2 × 1·5m.)   March–April*

Less spectacular than the foregoing but a good, hardy and distinctive evergreen with glossy-waxed leaves which set off to perfection the sprays of little white urns. Recent forms brought into cultivation such as 'Blush' and 'Christmas Cheer' have a decided pink flush to pedicel, calyx and even into the corolla, hence offering a new colour range to the genus. These are good in close detail but less effective at a distance. There is also an attractive form with variegated leaves. It grows slowly but is good for brightening a dark corner.

The hardiness of this species has been brought into a scarlet-leaved hybrid ('Wakehurst' is the other parent) which can be used where the basic *forrestii* gets too beaten up. This is the lovely and aptly named 'Forest Flame', whose new leaves begin scarlet, becoming pink and cream before turning green. In their early stages, of course, they are as frost-tender as any and need sensible help.

taiwanensis *6 − 8 × 6ft (2 − 2·5 × 2m.) March–April*

By a quirk of nomenclature this comes from the island of Formosa (Taiwan) while *Pieris formosa* is from the Eastern Himalayas: both geographers and botanists using the Latin *formosa* for beautiful. The Taiwan species is a quieter plant than the other but hardly less lovely. Growth becomes some- what tiered with dark green leaves setting off the half-erect panicles of flowers. Buds, brownish pink, are made in autumn and open so gradually that the plant seems to be 'on the move' all winter — a most heartening sight. Young growth is soft red and copper.

RHODODENDRON. This is the biggest genus, and most diverse in appearance, which we need to consider. There are some 800 wild species from all over the world (except Africa and South America) utilizing every habitat from exposed mountainside at great altitudes to deep sub-tropical jungles where humidity seldom falls below 100 per cent. Some of the high alpines never exceed a foot in height (though their flowers may be hugely out of all proportion to their bodies) while lowland species can reach full forest-tree proportions and are amongst the showiest plants in the world. Their colour-range almost spans the spectrum, with flowering times from January to August (a few make a second autumn flush as if the genus cannot bear not to offer something to every month of the year). They may be evergreen or deciduous — separating deciduous azaleas is convenient but has no botanical validity — with leaf-colour variation rivalling that of conifers, and size and texture brooking no comparison in diversity.

In addition to all this, hybridization and selection ever since the first Himalayan species were brought into cultivation in the early decades of the nineteenth century, has added perhaps many hundreds of more or less distinct plants. More appear every year.

Following now is a short list of some of the most beautiful (a highly subjective selection) members of the genus, species and hybrids. This may act as something of an aide-memoire but the only way to choose rhododendrons for one's own garden is to visit others to see what does well in one's own area (holiday visiting, from home in Northumberland, to the great Cornish gardens is not the same exercise at all), to see how they are used and to pick out the personally irresistable.

Hence the Northern Horticultural Society's Garden of Harlow Car at Harrogate, Yorkshire, Wisley and Windsor in Surrey, Exbury in Hampshire, Bodnant in North Wales and a host of other gardens from Inverewe in the far north west to Wakehurst Place in the south east can act as living local textbooks.

Small Rhododendrons   *2 – 5ft (600mm. – 1·5m.)*

These associate well, taking care of colour combinations with heaths and heathers, adding bulk and leaf-texture to the scene.

'Bric a Brac'. A charming hybrid which is light years away from the common conception of rhododendrons. It makes a small, open bush with wide-open white bells whose purity is enhanced by the bitter-chocolate anthers inside. Its parents, *R. moupinense* and *R. leucaspis*, both Himalayans, have equal charm. Planted as a trio, with protection from the east and half to three-quarters shade they give flower for several weeks — from mid February in some years — and overlap sufficiently to offer interesting hybrid versus species comparison.

'Cilpinense'. Another *moupinese* hybrid, this time with *R. ciliatum*, this makes a tidy dome of hair-fringed leaves covered in March with pink-flushed flowers. It makes an exquisite tub plant for a shady courtyard and as it matures the stems develop mahogany-coloured flaking bark.

mucronulatum often flowers in January when one might think it would be at risk, although the plant itself is laurel-hardy. Being deciduous, the sudden flush — in the protection of hamamelis, perhaps — is even more dramatic.

There is obviously a calculated risk in going in for any of these early flowerers but their small size makes it possible, when a flower-killing frost threatens, to rush out at dusk and cover one's favourite with a table-cloth. Sometimes it even helps.

x **praecox** shares the *ciliatum* parent. It is a semi-deciduous, rather upright plant, covering itself with rosy purple flowers in late February. An astonishingly strong colour for the season.

racemosum moves on the season into late March. It is remarkable, as the name suggests, in having bunches of pink flowers right up the stem, covering the plant for weeks.

scintillans is typical of several small near-blue species and hybrids, making domes of tiny scaly leaves which when in flower in early May change from green to blue. Often there is an autumn flush of flower as a bonus. These plants will take full sun but flower colour is enhanced and lasts longer in light birch shade. There is an FCC. (R.H.S. First Class Certificate) form to insist upon.

williamsianum. Even if it never flowered the nearly circular leaves with a petiole notch to make them heartshaped and the young bronze growths would make it desirable. Add to this in April the clear shell-pink bells and you have a particularly lovely plant.

yakushimanum. There is no doubt that this species from a Japanese off-island is destined to be brought into a range of hybrids. Meanwhile selections from the wild plants are splendid enough. They make low mushrooms of relatively large leaves and carry heads of pink buds which pale gradually to white. The new growths are bright silver and this indumentum is retained on the leaf reverses as dark brown suede.

Medium-sized Rhododendrons   *5 – 10ft (1·5 – 3m.)*

In this arbitrary group are literally hundreds of good plants. Here are one or two chosen to emphasize the diversity of the genus.

augustinii. In its best forms this is as near true blue as Rhododendrons can get, the purity of the colour being encouraged by shade. Leaves are small and the effect light and airy.

cinnabarinum. This, with its hybrids, is one of the great treats of the Rhododendron year. Leaves are bluish — in *Roylei* noticeably glaucous — and the flowers narrowly tubular in shape and texture, recalling those waxen bells of *Lapageria*. They are similarly pendulous so that the whole bush, perhaps 10 ft (3m.) high, cascades with dusky red, yellow, orange or deep plum-purple. The range is most diverse with 'Lady Chamberlain' and its forms, raised at Exbury in the 1930s; a visit to that garden in late May or early June makes imperative a stroll through 'Lady Chamberlain's Walk', where these plants tower up on all sides. Instant conversion, were there any doubt before, is inevitable.

griersonianum. The dangerously fierce pinks, reds and purples have been consciously avoided in this list and to maintain this exclusion yet to bring in the stronger colours this species is invaluable. It is very distinct, with long narrow leaves buff-woolly underneath, and in June carries lax heads of soft clear scarlet, a red with no blue in it. 'May Day', 'Tally Ho' and many other lovely hybrids have come from this plant. Any of them look superb in woodland where gleams of sun can light up the flowers like lamps illuminated from within.

lutescens repeats the small-leaf, open-habit type of *augustinii* with primrose flowers and bronzy young growths. The effect from a distance recalls corylopsis.

yunnanese has similar lightness of growth. Here the flowers are pink or white with dark spots, individually small, but highly effective in the mass. This is another excellent woodland plant: May-flowering.

Yellow is introduced particularly by two further Himalayans, *Rr. campylocarpum* and *Wardii*. Their hybrids such as, from the former, 'Carita' and 'Letty Edwards', and 'Hawk' and 'Jervis Bay' from the latter offer a range of soft shades often flushed with purple or pink.

Larger Rhododendrons.

It has already been mentioned that species such as *R. arboreum* can attain full forest tree size whilst those including *R. sinogrande*, although not making such tall plants are, in scale, amongst the most imposing things we can grow. The latter carries leaves up to 2½ feet in length in vast rosettes surmounted by football-sized heads of flowers. A magnificent sight indeed but fortunately perhaps, because of its intolerance of hard frost, not one for general planting. Nonetheless others, with leaves nearly as big such as *Rr. falconeri* and *fictolacteum* are much hardier and are seen in sheltered spots around the country. But they are so easily apt to dwarf their neighbours that effective use is not easy.

The best tall rhododendrons for woodland remain those with an open habit. Many are highly floriferous; others, by comparison with the prodigal Hardy Hybrids, may appear decidedly thin but it is just this habit — a branch flowering where it catches the sun, another not — that can suggest the authentic atmosphere of their Himalayan homes.

In this context mention must be made of one of Hooker's original Himalayan introductions dating back to 1849. Everything is good about *R. thomsonii*: smooth blue-green leaves, a trunk to rival *Arbutus andrachnoides*, blood-red flowers each in a green calyx, which remains ornamental after the corolla has fallen. It has passed on its attributes to many hybrids.

While *R. griffithianum* is lovely in south-west gardens (Arnold Forster[1] considered it 'King of all the species') it is in its many hybrids that it is generally appreciated. Where there is plenty of room the 'Loderi' forms are unsurpassed. Huge heads of pink or white flowers, each like a lily in size and scent, cover the plants.

Other Rhododendrons.

As has been obvious from the foregoing, gardens in mild areas enjoying also protection from wind can offer homes to a number of splendid plants which the rest of us can only enjoy vicariously. There is a still more tender group which are worth a mention here as tub plants for shady town courtyards if the protection of a cold house is available for November to April inclusive. Just two or three specimens, for example 'Lady Alice Fitzwilliam', 'Princess Alice' or *maddenii* with heavily scented white flowers and cinnamon bark add a definite touch of class. Surprisingly large plants will grow in a twelve-inch pot if well looked after.

Azaleas. It is usual to expect 'azaleas' to be deciduous and 'rhododendrons' to be evergreen but such apparent simplicity is not fully maintained. Nonetheless the biggest, most typical groups of azaleas do lose their leaves in winter and therefore often offer splendid autumn colour as an addition to their early summer effect.

The archetypal azalea is *Rhododendron luteum*, a lovely yellow, sweetly scented 6–8ft (2 × 2·5m.) plant from the Caucasus. It is so much at home here that it has become naturalized in several places in open woodland. Its gentle colour and open habit, fragrance and later autumn colour make it an invaluable acid-soil shrub. With other, mainly American species, it

[1]*Shrubs for the Milder Counties, Country Life, 1948.*

produced the Ghent Hybrid Azaleas, beginning in the 1830s. Most of these are in shades of yellow and soft orange. Delicate cream, pinks and pale apricots occur in the Occidentale Hybrids. These too are deliciously scented.

General lack of scent is a sad omission in the biggest groups, Knap Hill, Exbury and Mollis azaleas. Their superb heads of flowers in amazing shades of scarlet, vermilion, fiery reds and salmon pink make them inevitably highly considered. The display is truly remarkable but it is not being precious to state that careless juxtaposition of brilliant azalea colours with the bluish reds of evergreen rhododendrons produces an effect which must, at the kindest, be described as decidedly restless. Here is the great danger of the acid-soil shade-garden just as it is its great potential. Success in garden terms is not how kaleidoscopic an effect can be obtained — that is easier than falling off the proverbial log with these plants, but how satisfactory garden pictures can be built up to provide interest and beauty throughout the year. Hot colours, if they are to be used, must be separated and 'cooled' by the use of foliage plants or the palest shades.

With only a small garden to plant it might be thought that such aesthetic dangers are proportionately lessened. But as there are groups of dwarfish evergreen azaleas (Kaempferi, Kurume and so on) of equal brilliance it will be seen that problems of effective choice are common to all. Again, one must visit existing gardens to choose favourites and compose one's pictures in theory before putting them into practice. One man's dire mistake is another's keen pleasure and vice versa.

STEWARTIA. A lovely group of deciduous Camellia-relations enjoying edge-of-wood conditions. All have white flowers on large shrubs or small cherry-sized trees. As summer flowerers they are invaluable for giving late interest to the acid shrub garden. A small garden with shade and shelter could use a stewartia as a single specimen tree where habit, flower, autumn colour and ornamental flaking bark combine and succeed each other, enlivening season after season.

pseudocamellia   *25 × 15ft (7·5 × 4·5m.)*   *July–August*

This is perhaps the best for general use, its white flowers fleeting but repeating over a long period. *Koreana* is similar with wider-opening flowers, while those of *malacodendron* are pink- or purple-flushed at the base and rather resemble Eucryphia flowers.

STYRAX. Valuable summer-flowering large shrubs or small trees enjoying the same conditions as Stewartias. They are known in the United States, very suitably, as Snowbells.

japonica   *20 × 15ft (6 × 4·5m.)*   *June*

The most generally available and perhaps the best. It needs a position in semi-shade where there is room for its elegantly tiered branch-pattern to develop fully and be appreciated from a distance. The myriad flowers need closer inspection and as they hang from the branches the plant is ideally placed where a path can run underneath and one can look up into the layers of whiteness.

Few, if any, of the other species are likely to be available but *obassia*, with fine big round leaves, and the somewhat similar *hemsleyana* could be sought out.

VACCINIUM. An invaluable genus for the heather garden and associating with Rhododendrons, beneath which many are happy as an understory. Our own Cowberry belongs here (*V. vitis-idaea* which makes good shade ground cover) as do the blueberries (*Vv. corymbosum* and *angustifolium*) widely cultivated in the United States. It is one of the few soft fruits happy on very acid soils. In half sun its autumn colour is dramatic.

There are several good dwarf Vacciniums, all of which associate well with heaths and enjoy shady banks, if reasonable moisture is available. Of the bigger species the following are particularly desirable.

glauco-album. This reaches 5 feet in height with glossy leaves whose undersides are bloomed with bright milk-white. This same bloom covers the bracts to the pink flowers and, later, the black fruits. A most distinctive plant.

padifolium is the Madeiran whortleberry. It comes from high altitudes and is thus relatively hardy here in shelter. The flowers, amongst the netted leaves, are green but carried in sufficient quantity to make a show, as are, later, the purple fruits.

virgatum. Another American, known there as the 'Rabbiteye Blueberry'. It has a more open, frond-like habit than the others, making a lighter effect. Pink flowers are succeeded by black fruits. Autumn colour is good.

ZENOBIA pulverulenta   *4 × 3ft (1·2 × 1m.)   June*

A most charming small shrub thriving in the semi-shade of bigger calcifuges. It has spikes of lily-of-the-valley flowers in late June and July and conspicuously white-dusted leaves. Coming from the eastern United States it is perfectly hardy and should be sought out and used more.

6 Shrubs for Shade on Limy Soils

As has already been discussed, generations of deciduous leaf-fall in woodland gradually build up a soil with a high humus content which because of its organic origin is almost bound to have an acid reaction, even above a limy substrate. It follows that plants directly associated with such conditions in the wild are evolutionarily adapted not only to succeed in shade but also on acid soils. Some groups must be described as obligate calcifuges: the rhododendrons and heathers, indeed the vast majority of their family, the Ericaceae, are examples: they cannot take lime.

There seems to be no such group of shrubs on the other side of the fence: calcicole must be taken as *lime-accepting* rather than the often used phrase 'lime-loving'. The significance of this is that the following shrubs, offering a wide range of splendid effects for shady gardens on limy soils can, with few exceptions, also be grown in a lower-than-7 pH.

ARALIA. The 'Devil's Walking Stick' is a satisfactory name for these plants in winter when they show nothing but 10-ft (3-m.) high spiny poles but their other name, 'Angelica Tree', is better in summer. Then the rosettes of splendid dissected leaves, very much like those of the herb (though in no way related) makes a fine pattern. Above these there comes a cloud of tiny white flowers in August and September. The species most available is *A. elata*: its variegated forms make good specimen plants in a shady corner of the lawn.

AUCUBA. Strong evergreens of considerable potential; the 'spotted laurels' succeed in the shadiest places. Their acceptance of difficult positions has done their image no good, causing relegation to the screening of lavatories in the seedier public parks and similar valuable but unexciting roles. Aucubas are dioecious and thus at least one male plant must be grown in the vicinity of females if they are to fruit.

japonica   *8 × 8ft (2·5 × 2·5m.)   April*

Selected forms are usually grown for their individual virtues of size, leaf or fruit.

—**borealis** and '**Crassifolia**' (both male) are dwarfer than most.

—'**Crotonifolia**' (male) is the best form of the spotted laurel, with striking variegation. Even here, however, the irregularity of the gold blotches may make it unacceptable to those who insist upon more definite patterns, for whom the yellow-edged 'Sulphurea' will be more acceptable. The variegation of both pales in deep shade.

—'**Salicifolia**'. A lovely plant with long, narrow lustrous leaves and copious crops of scarlet berries. These ripen after Christmas and hang on until flowering time the following May.

BAMBOOS. It is perhaps sensible to group several genera here which combine together under the common and evocative name. Bamboos are woody-stemmed grasses, elegant in habit, with sprays of long narrow evergreen leaves. A number are admirable in shade where moisture is enjoyed but bad drainage abhorred.

The bigger species make thick screens for the edge of woodland, reaching 15 feet (4·5m.) or so in height. Included here are *Arundinaria anceps* and *A. graminea* (this actually does *best* in shade). Less rampantly vigorous are *A. murieliae* and *A. nitida*, both up to 10 feet (3m.) in height but of such delicate form that they appear almost weightless. In association with broadleaved foliage plants, *Fatsia* or *Viburnum rhytido-phyllum*, with Bergenia at the base, a fine garden picture can be built up. Equally lovely is a single clump: in a large shady courtyard or town garden either of these species do well in large tubs — Chinese pickled-cabbage jars are ideal; some, indeed, are decorated with a bamboo motif which the plant picks up.

There are also dwarf bamboos, which run about to form

thick ground cover under shrubs. There is a danger of their being over enthusiastic and so they should be introduced under already established plants rather than with young contemporaries. *Arundinaria pumila* and *Sasa veitchii* (ADS) with broad leaves, white-edged in winter, are examples. These two make ground cover in broad swathes; very restrained by comparison and rather tight in habit, is the attractive *Arundinaria variegata* with pale-striped leaves.

Unless draught-shelter or solid visual screening is required the beauty of bamboos is enhanced by a regular thinning of the clumps, cutting out annually a few old stems. At their present retail price, home-grown bamboo canes are a useful addition to the garden economy.

BERBERIS. A huge genus of generally prickly growth offering both spring flower and autumn berry. The best flowerers, however, are usually the most inconspicuous fruiters and vice versa. Only a few of the best are dealt with here: unless otherwise stated they are evergreen.

calliantha   *3 − 4 × 3ft (1 − 1·2 × 1m.)   May*

A charming tidy dome of a bush with a definite 'presence'. Stems are at first pink and the leaves are beautifully white-bloomed beneath. The hanging flowers are amongst the largest of the genus, pale primrose-yellow followed by dark purple fruits.

darwinii   *6 − 8 × 6ft (2 − 2·5 × 2m.)   April–May*

Another Chilean, suitably commemorating Charles Darwin who discovered it on his 'Beagle' voyage. The dark foliage becomes almost hidden by bright orange flowers. Sometimes the grape-black fruits are produced in sufficient quantities to make an autumn show.

linearifolium.   *5 − 6 × 5ft (1·5 − 2 × 1·5m.)   April–May*

Again from Chile, but from higher altitudes than *darwinii*, with which it hybridizes to give *B. x lologensis*. It is naturally a woodland plant, with flowers of a truly startling orange-red. Not to be placed in sight of anything pink.

x stenophylla.   *6 − 8 × 8ft (2 − 2·5 × 2·5m.)   April*

Another *darwinii* hybrid, making a wide plant with arching growth covered in yellow flowers. It makes a good semi-formal hedge. Several forms varying in size and flower colour are available.

thunbergii.   *4 × 4ft (1·2 × 1·2m.)   May*

The yellow flowers make little show but the autumn effect of flame-coloured deciduous foliage and scarlet berries is superb. '*Atropurpurea*' is its invaluable purple-leaved form, but not for heavy shade. Rather taller than the type.

wilsonae   *3 × 4ft (1 × 1·2m.)   May*

Like other deciduous barberries from the Orient this is only suitable for half-shade. It makes low mounds of blue-green leaves which colour well in autumn as the fruits ripen to shades of coral and crimson. Several fine hybrids have been named, larger in size and even more prodigal in fruit, including 'Barbarossa', 'Bountiful' and x *rubrostilla*.

BUXUS. The common box, while happy in full sun even on thin chalk soils as at Box Hill in Surrey, is one of the very few shrubs to grow well in the dense shade of beech trees. It is one of the best hedge-plants for shade: a distinctive scent is particularly evident after rain, which is loved by some, hated by others.

sempervirens ADS   *10 − 15 × 10ft (3 − 4·5 × 3m.)*

Many forms are available with green or variegated leaves — the former being better in shade. 'Suffruticosa' is the dwarf box used for edging beds in formal gardens.

CHAENOMELES. On limy soils the Japanese quinces take something of the place of camellias in their range of early flower colour. Semi-double as well as single forms exist, and most give a bonus of small yellow quinces in autumn from which a distinctive preserve can be made.

japonica   *2 − 3 × 2ft (600 − 900 × 600mm.)   April*

A small twiggy bush with brilliant flame-orange flowers anticipating the colour of the subsequent preserve. Keep clear from pink flowering currant out at the same time.

speciosa   *3 − 4 × 4 − 5ft (1 − 1·2 × 1·2 − 1·5m.)   March–May*

It is this group that is commonly, and confusingly, called 'japonica'. In the moister west their wood fails in shade to ripen enough to flower well but in the east open ground plants under other shrubs do well as do wall-trained specimens (which can get quite high) even facing north. Colours range from white ('Nivalis') through pink ('Phyllis Moore') to dark red ('Simonii'), with most intermediate shades occurring as well. 'Simonii' is a low-growing plant: it is good under a window where taller things would be inappropriate: it gives good early flower in a spot facing south which is shaded in summer by deciduous trees.

Crosses between the two species listed are known as *C. x superba* and also come in a range of fine cultivars: some pick up the orange tint of *japonica*. Amongst the best are 'Knap Hill Scarlet' and 'Rowallane', a lovely blood red.

Chaenomeles may take time to settle down to flower well, but having done so are highly rewarding.

CISTUS. ADS It may seem paradoxical to list for shade these archetypal Mediterraneans, the sun-roses. But in fact, as one sees them at home in secondary maquis, they appear not only in the full glare of the sun but also in association with taller evergreens, Kermes Oak, Phillyrea and Lentisk. On a quick draining, light soil we in Britain can repeat this, at least in the south, with the hardier species and cultivars such as

x. **aguilari**	5 × 4ft (1·5 × 1·2m.) June	white	
'Betty Tauderin'	4 × 4ft (1·2 × 1·2m.) June	dark pink	
x **cyprius**	5 × 4ft (1·5 × 1·2m.) June	white with	
		maroon blotch	
'Silver Pink'	2 × 3ft (600 × 900mm.) June	pale pink	
x. **skanbergii**	3 × 3ft (1 × 1m.) June	pale pink	

This last is highly aromatic and the scent wafts on the air, a real fragrance of Mediterranean hillsides even in winter.

Other shrubs from the same areas such as Lavender, Colutea, Halimium can succeed in such positions in dry shade under specimen trees where the light concentration is relatively high.

CONIFERS. As with bamboos it is convenient to list together those conifers most happy in shade conditions. Because of their generally dark demeanour, soaking up light as sponges soak water, their use in shady spots is limited. The effect is too sombre, yet to give evergreen bulk and shelter to the base of an otherwise tall copse of deciduous trees is often desirable, for within such shelter more exciting things can grow. And as focal points at the side of steps or as ground cover on banks, several of the prostrate junipers are as useful in shade as in sun.

Many conifers grow in almost pure stands in their native habitats and hence, to ensure regeneration, their saplings are adapted to tolerate shade to a remarkable degree. Thus the giant fir, *Abies grandis*, can be considered for this very use as an evergreen nurse, although it may have to be removed later, if space is limited, when its charges cease to be children and its job is done. Similarly the elegant Western Hemlock (*Tsuga heterophylla*) has much to offer to the shade-gardener: it is surprising that such an ornamental plant has remained almost entirely the possession of the forester, who finds it ideal for bearing shade under the mature trees which it will one day succeed. More generally, however, the garden value of conifers is as specimen plants where their distinctive shape and texture can be individually appreciated. Here, therefore, although many conifers could be tentatively listed for woodland use, only those most proved are described.

CEPHALOTAXUS. There are relatively fewer evergreen shrubs that are happy in shade than deciduous ones and proportionately even fewer conifers: their habit is usually to provide the shade-*giving* layer. But the plum-yews, a small group from Eastern Asia, are exceptions to the rule. All are yew-like shrubs or small trees with rather bigger leaves held in elegant fronds, and purplish fruits which rather resemble ripe olives in size and colour. The two species available are visually pretty close. *C. fortunii* is from China, while *C. harringtonia* is Japanese. (A chemical extract from the latter, Harringtonine, is, incidentally, currently being tested as an anti-cancer agent.) In the garden these are admirable shade-tolerant evergreens, greatly underused.

JUNIPERS. The prostrate junipers (the tree-sized species have little to offer us here) are plants of open moors, downs and shorelines. They are thus not plants for under-tree shade, understandably being intolerant of drip. Yet, as already mentioned, courtyard shade, open to the sky, is acceptable to several useful plants.

These are the species and forms of *J. conferta*, green and prickly, *J. horizontalis*, especially eye-catching in blue-green types such as 'Bar Harbor', and *J. sabina* whose *tamariscifolia* is particularly good. *J.* x *media* has produced the most useful juniper of all in 'Pfitzerana'. As the invaluable Hillier's *Manual* so rightly states it 'is a friend of the landscape gardener, it never lets him down, it marries the formal into the informal, it embellishes his layout and hides his errors'. The strong 45 degree branches with pendulous tips make a fine pattern and though commonly seen do not become a cliché if sensibly sited. There are several other *J.* x *media* forms, all worth consideration. *Taxus baccata*, our native yew, has innumerable garden uses from classic hedging to formal sentinels and effective ground cover. The fleshy red or yellow fruits are often carried, on pollinated female trees, in sufficient quantity to make quite a show, but the birds seldom permit it to last for long.

In its normal form the effect of yew is so dark as to be almost black, especially in shade where light is already scarce. Here the golden 'Elegantissima' is admirable and though in deepest shade much colour is lost the ultimate effect is not as dark as the type. The Irish Yew is the one which maintains an upright habit, while 'Cavendishii' and 'Repandens' make splendid horizontal ground cover. In heavy shade these are much more successful than the prostrate junipers. It should be added that yews well-cared for do not deserve their reputation for slowness of growth.

CORNUS. Many of the calcicole dogwoods are grown especially for the bright winter bark of their young growth. Unfortunately this is so reduced in shade as to be of little use for that purpose. However, the variegated forms of *Cornus alba* are well worth their space. 'Elegantissima' and 'Spaethii', white-striped and yellow-striped respectively, make a bright splash throughout summer and their foliage is admirable for cutting.

CORYLUS. Coppice hazel is the classic plant under standard oak trees and its myriad catkins waving in a February breeze above the shooting bluebell spears is one of the most heartening sights of incipient spring. If the plant already exists in a woodland garden it must be cherished. If not a few might be planted, one to be cut down each year to supply the now inordinately expensive bean-poles, and to maintain the coppice form.

avellana   *10 × 15ft (3 − 4·5m.)   February*

Our native hazel. For a small garden or in a dominant position in a courtyard the Corkscrew Hazel ('Contorta') can be used as a specimen plant. In flower it is a splendid sight.

maxima   *10 × 15ft (3 − 4·5m.)   February*

The Filbert, bigger in all its parts but just as attractive. The purple-leaved form adds a sombre yet luscious note to any planting of foliage shrubs. Good with golden variegated things such as Sambucus but one must beware of the dangerously heavy late-summer effect.

COTONEASTER. One of our most valuable genera, offering shade-accepting evergreens varying from low carpeters to small trees. Most have white or pink flushed flowers in early summer followed by prodigious crops of, usually red, fruit in autumn. Often this holds on for several months.

Low-growing cotoneasters, *less than 3ft (1m.)*

dammeri. A lovely ground hugging shrub which follows exactly the contours beneath it. Dark evergreen leaves studded with red fruit.

horizontalis. The commonest and still the best with dramatic herringbone pattern branches. This species is deciduous and its leaves colour as brightly as its berries. Against a wall it can get quite high: an admirable dark courtyard or north wall plant. There is a pretty variegated form, though slow growing and mean in fruit.

microphyllus. Equally good as ground cover or to plant at the top of a retaining wall. Curtains of foliage will then descend to the ground, pink and white in June, scarlet in November, glossy green for the rest of the year.

salicifolius repens. A low-growing form of a much bigger plant (see below) which differs greatly in effect from the other carpeters. The strong arching growths have large leaves 2 – 3 inches (50 – 75mm.) and carry heavy bunches of fruit.

Medium growers, *5 – 8ft (1·5 – 2·5m.)*

conspicuus 'Decorus'. Although often described as a dwarf this plant gradually builds up a high mound of arching branches. It is particularly free with both flower and fruit.

harrovianus. Another lovely arching shrub which would be worth growing for its flower even if no fruit followed. In fact the second display is particularly good and admirably late.

Large cotoneasters, *8 – 12ft + (2·5 – 4m. +)*

lacteus. A strong 'weighty' plant. The leathery leaves are white-felted beneath and set off huge heads of fruit.

salicifolius. The narrow willow-like leaves are carried on elegant arching branches which bend further with the weight of its fruits. A most graceful plant at all times, it can act as the shrub layer in an open woodland stratification or be trained up to near-tree size itself. It has been used as a parent in many hybrids which are given the group name of

x **watereri**. Of the named clones, good ones with red fruit include 'John Waterer' and 'Cornubia'. In gardens where birds are more than usually greedy and leave little time for visual enjoyment of berries 'Pink Champagne' and 'Exburiensis' are admirable: our feathered friends wait around for them to ripen to edible red which, happily, they never do. Both gradually change from yellow to pink.

DANAË racemosa. This unusual liliaceous plant is closely related to Butcher's Broom but its growth is as graceful as the other is stiff. Here arching stems of narrow shiny leaves spring from the ground to 3 feet or so. Under the name of Alexandrian Laurel it is sometimes sold as cut foliage — it lasts extremely well in water — but is hardly ever seen in gardens.

DAPHNE. Some of our most desirable garden shrubs belong here. Tidy growth, earliness of flower and intense fragrance are hallmarks. The small high alpines are not plants for shade but some are natural woodlanders.

bholua.   *6 − 8 × 5ft (2 − 2·5 × 1·5m.)   February–April*

One of the most promising of recent shrub introductions, this is likely to be the biggest daphne known. It makes a vigorous vertical bush covered in early spring with white, purple-backed flowers. Not averse to lime but a good leafy soil is needed.

laureola.   *3 × 2ft (900 × 600mm.)   February*

Our native Spurge Laurel comes from dark woods often on damp clay soils. It is not a showy plant but the shiny evergreen leaves under which the clusters of green, yellow-eyed and scented flowers hide make it a quietly distinctive plant.

mezereum   *3 − 4 × 3ft (1 − 1·2 × 1m.)   February–March*

The well-known deciduous Mezereon is another woodland native but only rarely found wild. It does best in cool spots on retentive soil but is erratic in length of life; sometimes an apparently happy plant will flower well and then quietly subside. Perhaps it is naturally not long-lived — certainly it is a martyr to a debilitating virus and should be regularly sprayed against aphid vectors.

The usual form is a strong purple — rather the colour of *Rhododendron* x *praecox* and there is a more vertically growing white form ('Alba'). The type has red fruits, while 'Alba' has yellow. Both are highly poisonous to man but irresistible to birds. Net a branch and sow as soon as ripe to keep good young plants growing.

odora   *3 − 4 × 4ft (1 − 1·2 × 1·2m.)   February–April*

A plant that no shady (or indeed any) garden should be without. Intensely lemon-scented flower clusters, crystalline-white with pink reverses, end every shoot and are held for weeks. Invaluable for late-winter posies.

The form with yellow-edged leaves, 'Aureomarginata' is, surprisingly, both hardier and stronger in growth than the wild green species.

DAPHNIPHYLLUM macropodum.   *8 × 8ft (2·5 × 2·5m.)*
June

If anyone on chalky soil hankers after rhododendrons (though he would do better to move) this is the plant to grow. Splendid pale green leaves with purplish stalks make it a striking foliage plant but, as it is a Euphorbia, the flowers are nothing to write home about.

DEUTZIA. Foaming white or pink flowers in June and July are the characteristic of this easily grown group. Not for deep tree shade but most happily on the north side of buildings, lighting up their spot. Some of the flowered growth should be cut out each year to keep an open bush: one must take care not to snap off new growths when so doing.

Among the best of the bigger Deutzias, attaining 6 feet or so, are x *elegantissima* and x *kalmiiflora* (the individual flowers really are like Kalmia, impossible on a limy soil). Both are white, pink-flushed. *Pulchra* from Taiwan is brilliant white. For small gardens or narrow borders the x *rosea* group is ideal.

ELAEAGNUS pungens   *10 × 10ft (3 × 3m.)   October*

A fine evergreen, good for building up shelter in half shade. The flowers are small but strongly scented. Its variegated forms

1 *Clematis* 'Nelly Moser'. An old favourite whose flowers maintain their colour best in shade.

2 *Lonicera tragophylla* has 4-inch long trumpets of clear yellow. It is perhaps the best honeysuckle for a fully shaded wall.

3 *Helleborus abschasicus.* All Lenten Roses are among the best garden plants for shady positions.

4 The exquisite but fleeting flowers of *Paeonia mlokosewitschii* last
longer in dappled shade.

5 Aroids in leaf and flower are always of interest. *Arisaema candidissima* is one of the most beautiful.

6 Few shrubs can display flowers and fruits at the same time. *Hypericum* 'Elstead' is an exception.

'Maculata' (gold leaves, green-edged) and the newer 'Gilt Edge' are amongst our brightest foliage plants and maintain the effect in shade. Good for cutting throughout the winter.

x **ebbingii** is a hybrid of the above: from its other parent (*macrophylla*) it inherits fine silvery backs to its leaves. A splendid rapid growing evergreen.

EUONYMUS. Although the bigger deciduous spindle-berries accept the sort of light shade our own conspicuous spindle bush gets in a hedgerow, with more than this their growth becomes thin and few fruits are produced. The resultant plant is pretty pointless. However, in a couple of the evergreen species we have some of the best shade shrubs available.

fortunei. Although the leaves are oval and about 3 inches (75mm.) long, habit and behaviour of this Chinese plant is like that of ivy: it makes good ground cover or will climb by aerial roots if support is available. Also like ivy until it develops an arborescent form no flower or fruit is produced. Thus its use in shade is expressly as evergreen ground clothing on banks and under trees.

More common in cultivation is the slightly smaller-leaved subspecies *radicans* with similar attributes. This has several extremely valuable striped forms which will brighten up the darkest spot. The best are the suitably named 'Silver Queen' and 'Silver and Gold' which are as good grown as single specimens as in broad swathes.

japonicus ADS   *10 × 6ft (3 × 2m.)*

This dense evergreen, like a particularly lustrous privet, is particularly good near the sea. It is thus valuable as the low-level wind-filter under shelter-belt trees and able to take much more frost than the Olearia and Pittosporum used for this purpose in the mild south west. The white variegated form 'Albomarginatus' is the best of the striped kinds.

nanus   *3in. × 2ft (80 × 600mm.)*

A tiny semi-evergreen for ground cover. Thin-leaved bulbs, such as crocuses, will come through it happily.

FATSIA ADS   *8 × 6ft (2·5 × 2m.)   September–November*

One of the most striking plants we can grow, with huge hand-like leaves, evergreen and glossy. As a common house-plant it is often, wrongly, known as 'Castor-oil plant'. In the garden it is a marvellous courtyard-corner plant, always looking statuesque and accepting neglect and any soil type with impunity. The great heads of ivy-like, ivory-coloured flowers are a great draw for late-flying insects and, as they gradually turn into green and then black fruits, remain eye-catching until late spring. Self-sown seedlings are not uncommon. The white edged variegated form is less robust.

An extraordinary bigeneric hybrid between Fatsia and Irish Ivy is x *Fatshedera lizei*. Intermediate between the parents it makes marvellous layered ground cover. A single plant in an urn looks well in a deeply shady corner.

FORSYTHIA. The brilliant spring effect is one that everybody knows. In isolation it can even be too much of a good thing. In shade, however, flower is apt to be less solid and growth more open, creating a much more elegant effect.

giraldiana   *8 × 6ft (2·5 × 2m.)   February–March*

Pale yellow flowers on a graceful bush. It is usually the first to flower.

ovata   *4 × 4ft (1·2 × 1·2m.)   March*

This little bush is not far behind and is ideal to add its soft yellow to plantings of spring heathers.

suspensa   *10 × 10ft (3 × 3m.)   March–April*

In the open, with space, this makes a great fountain like a golden Roman candle firework. It is one of the best shrubs to train on a north wall.

There are several big-flowered hybrids of which 'Beatrix Farrand', 'Spectabilis' and 'Lynwood' are perhaps the best. The fact that forsythias are common and easily grown should not obscure their great beauty. If thought can be given to providing, where possible, a dark background and good associated planting at their feet, an altogether more dramatic garden picture can be built up than is usually seen.

FUCHSIA. While the numerous hybrids are invaluable stand-bys for the cool greenhouse, several species and their forms are ideal for shady courtyards and for giving late summer interest under early-flowering shrubs. They have the admirable facility of being able to behave like herbaceous perennials in areas or seasons too cold to permit overwintering wood. It is not necessary to cut everything down: earlier flowers on taller growth are obtained from last year's twigs.

magellanica. In spite of its delicate habit this fine South American is able to withstand full seaside blast. On a shady wall it will get high and develop thick flaking trunks, dripping with red and purple flowers for months on end. The common 'Riccartonii' is similar but bigger. There is also a very pretty variegated-leaved form, rather less hardy, and a particularly desirable type called 'Versicolor'. Framing the usual-coloured flowers, the foliage is purplish grey (rather like that of *Rosa rubrifolia*) with occasional pink flecks. Watch must be kept for ordinary green shoots.

Of the hybrids all are so easily propagated from cuttings that there is little risk to one's pocket to leave plants outside heaped over in winter with a free-draining mulch. Several, such as 'Mrs Popple', 'Mme Cornelisen' and 'Tom Thumb' are particularly recommended as hardy types but I have no doubt that most of the others would do as well.

GRISELINIA littoralis. While this fine New Zealand evergreen is useless in cold gardens, in most maritime areas (and London) it makes useful under-tree wind shelter. Branches of the roundish apple-green leaves make good cut foliage. Variegated forms are available; that known as 'Dixon's Cream' is the most distinct.

HEBE. A big genus of evergreens, again mainly from New Zealand, of what used to be called shrubby Veronicas. With such a distribution it is obvious that many resent hard frost (and show it by dying): the most striking in flower are in general the most tender. While all seem happy in full sun many are equally so in half to three-quarter shade. Drought is apt to be resented yet Hebe 'Pagei' makes perfect mats of grey-glaucous ground cover under Holm Oaks — surely the most unwelcoming home to be offered to any plant. Other easy-to-please hebes include the following but many more, big and small, would repay experiment.

albicans   *2 × 2ft (600 × 600mm.)   July*

A good hummock of glaucous leaves covered with small spikes of white flowers.

'Autumn Glory'   *2 × 2ft (600 × 600mm.)   July–October*

Purplish foliage and flowers to match over a long period.

x **franciscana**   *3 × 4ft (1 × 1·2m.)   January–December*

This is the ubiquitous 'Veronica' of every Cornish garden: it takes full exposure and also some shade. Few plants can honestly claim such a flowering period. 'Blue Gem' is the best form and the hardiest. Old plants of this were commonly killed in the winter of 1978–9 yet seedlings survived.

hulkeana   *1·5 × 2ft (450 × 600mm.)   May*

Unlike the usual bottle-brush hebe spike, here the soft blue flowers — each just like a speedwell — are carried in big loose panicles. It grows on shady rock ledges in the South Island of New Zealand and seems hardier in fact than in reputation. *H. fairfieldii* may be the same thing.

'Midsummer Beauty'   *5 × 5ft (1·5 × 1·5m.)   June–September*

By far the best hebe in flower for general garden effect. Long lavender spikes continue for months. Not for deepest shade but takes quite a lot.

salicifolia   *6 – 8 × 6ft (2 – 2·5 × 2m.)   June–August*

Willow-like leaves and white flowers. These are carried in long pendulous spikes and the whole plant becomes a cascade for weeks. The warm brown seed capsules look well in winter.

speciosa   *5 × 5ft (1·5 × 1·5m.)   June_November*

The type species of many showy selections and hybrids, none very hardy. However, cuttings root easily and it is simple to keep replacements. Good in shady courtyards in the ground or in tubs.

HYDRANGEA. In addition to the well-known mop-head hydrangea, so much a feature of potted arrangements at summer celebrations, the genus contains several other excellent shade-needing and shade-tolerant plants. It might be mentioned here that the mop-heads are garden forms in which many of the fertile flowers in the centre of a naturally flat head have become sterile, developing the extravagant sepals normally possessed only by the outer ring.

cinerea   *3 × 4ft (1 × 1·2m.)   June–July*

A North American species with greyish woolly leaves and heads of white flowers: the form 'Sterilis' is best for garden decoration, associating well both with herbaceous plants or taller shrubs.

paniculata *5 − 6 × 5ft (1·5 − 2 × 1·5m.)   July–September*

As the name suggests the flower heads are triangular rather than the typical round or flat head. Well fed and hard pruned (after a framework has been built up) like a buddleia in spring this produces heads of monumental size. (But then they need support: for normal garden decoration a gentle thinning of growth is sufficient.) They are white and darken gently to pink. For windy, cold gardens the smaller 'Praecox' is a wiser choice.

quercifolia *6 − 8 × 5ft (2 − 2·5 × 1·5m.)   July*

A shrub layer plant of the tulip-tree woodland of the south-east United States. Not exciting in flower it comes into its own with dramatic autumn leaf colour.

sargentiana *6 − 8 × 4ft (2 − 2·5 × 1·2m.)   July–August*

Reminiscent in habit of Aralia with its gawky stem pattern entirely hidden by great summer leaves. The flower heads are near-blue with white outside ray-florets which gradually change to green. Another woodland plant, good too for exotic effect in a moist shady courtyard.

villosa *6 × 6ft (2 × 2m.)   July–August*

A most lovely plant for half or full shade, but intolerant of drought. The blue-purple flower heads, above velvety leaves, have a warm, glowing quality. This is one of the species which could be chosen for a carefully selected group to provide shade-interest under and around a specimen tree.

The common garden hydrangeas are based around two Japanese species, *H. macrophylla* and the smaller *H. serrata*. It is the former which has given us the splendid florists' 'Hortensia' mop-head hydrangeas.

In most areas they are definitely better in shade, under taller shrubs, north walls and they are especially valuable on acid soils to extend the season of interest when a predominance of planting has been given to the earlier *Ericaceae*. Here, many of the hortensias take on shades of brilliant blue while these same cultivars on limy soils are pink. Where soil is neutral, by the frequent use of an aluminium sulphate-based 'bluing powder', blueness can be artificially maintained. But it is a mistake to try this with a high pH: the resultant miserable purplish tints are seldom of much virtue: better to enjoy the pink and the white.

In mild and humid areas these plants can make huge bushes 10 feet high and as much through. Half that size is more common. It should be mentioned that their habit of making next year's flower buds in the previous autumn and being tempted into growth by our frequent false springs causes the loss of these buds in areas susceptible to late frosts. Avoid especially an eastern exposure.

While one may have success with a hydrangea bought for house decoration and subsequently put out, it should be realised that different cultivars have been developed for the two jobs. Amongst the best for outside are:

Mop-heads

'Europa', dark pink
'Goliath', pink or purplish blue
'Madame Emile Mouillière', white with pink or blue eye
'Marechal Foch', bright pink or gentian blue

Lacecaps

Closer to the wild species are forms with only an outside ring of big infertile flowers. The flat heads can be very striking.

'Blue Wave', central fertile flowers, blue with the outside flowers pink or blue
'Mariesii', mid-pink or clear medium blue
'Maculata' and **'Tricolor'**, are both blue variegated-leaved forms: the latter also flowers well.
'Preziosa', is a cross between *H. macrophylla* and *H. serrata*. The influence of the latter keeps it small — to 4 feet (1·2m.) or so — while the former provides the ball-like heads of flowers which open pale and darken to purple as autumn approaches (such a colour change is common with hydrangeas) and many

remain ornamental throughout winter, especially under hoar
frost, maintaining inflorescence structure although the flowers
have become papery and brown. The *serratas* grow rather
meanly on dry soils.

'**Bluebird**' is a low-growing form with round infertile heads:
purple on lime and greenish-blue, a lovely shade, on acid soils.

'**Grayswood**' is a lace-cap alternative with blue central flowers
surrounded by white ray-florets which gradually darken,
through pink to red.

HYPERICUM. The St John's Worts make up a bright, happy
group of shrubs untainted by any hint of guile: their open
full-face cups of gold are centred with a conspicuous fuzz of
stamens. All take half-shade, some much more.

androsaemum   *2 − 3 × 2ft (600 − 900 × 600mm.)*
June–August

Our native Tutsan is one of the best small shrubs for under-tree
(or indeed any) shade. The heads of small flowers are succeeded by red fleshy capsules soon turning black and dry. In this
state they hold on for months.

calycinum *1 × infinity (300mm.)   July–September*

The Rose of Sharon has the finest flowers ('Rowallane' not
excepted) of any Hypericum. Three-inch wide cups with a great
brush of stamens stud the plant: a dry bank in shade or sun even
on pure chalk becomes a carpet of gold. But so invasive is the
plant that it must be used with care: under trees and mature
shrubs it can be happily introduced but newly planted things
will not enjoy such competition.

x **inodorum** 'Elstead' has Tutsan in its parentage but is an
altogether brighter and more desirable plant. Here the fruits do
not blacken but remain vividly pink. The succession of bloom is
such that fruit and flower appear together in a positively fair-
ground miscellany.

patulum Around this name are grouped some splendid garden shrubs making symmetrical domes of shining leaves and bright gold flowers. They vary in height from about 2ft (600mm.) in x *moseranum* (which has the Rose of Sharon as its other parent but does not inherit its rampageousness) to 'Hidcote' attaining 6ft (2m.) or so. *Forrestii* and 'Gold Cup' are intermediate in size. All are as wide as they are high.

'Rowallane' *6 × 4ft (2 × 1·2m.)*   *August–December*

A magnificent St. John's Wort for a sheltered corner. The great gold flowers are bowl-shaped and of an almost waxy texture: often they are carried until Christmas.

ILEX. As holly, with ivy, is our commonest evergreen woodlander it follows that, with garden forms and hybrids, we have a splendid shade-tolerant group. But native holly can attain full tree size although, by clipping and pruning it can be kept much smaller (Christmas needs have an effect here). As specimen plants, as wind shelter or screening under taller trees, hollies are admirable.

aquifolium (common holly) and x *altaclarensis* (its bigger-leaved hybrid) have produced dozens of desirable forms varying in habit, leaf size and shape, amount of spininess and type and colour of variegation. Since holly is dioecious there has been an obvious tendency to try to select each in both male and female forms. Yellow berries, which are left much longer than the red by the birds, are also produced. So great is the range, then, that it is pointless to do any more than name a couple of favourites.

'Golden King', in spite of its name, is a fine free-fruiting female with yellow-splashed leaves. 'Silver Sentinal' is well named as is 'Camelliifolia': both fruit well. But, of course, with every three or four of these a male clone must be provided for pollination (unlike domestic hens, the customary help is necessary). Careful examination of an existing but non-fruiting holly in flower will show whether it is itself male or a female lacking a pollinator. While hollies will take poor chalky soils it should be emphasised that they respond to humus and hearty feeding in the early years: without this growth can be depressingly slow.

Visitors to the eastern United States are always impressed by a range of native hollies which hold their fruit almost into spring. Some, forms of *I. verticillata* and *I. opaca*, are available here but do less well: they need more sun and lime-free soils.

China, Japan and the Himalayas also offer some fine hollies but so far in this country they have remained the preserve of specialists. Many make good shade plants to add to our own species but the latter still carries the crown.

KERRIA japonica. The bright butter-yellow rather ragged flowers of this cottage-garden shrub always make a good spring show. It is the double form we usually see, often against a shady wall. But the type with single potentilla-like flowers is a more elegant plant only 4–5ft (1·2 – 1·5m.) tall: its variegated form is very thin.

LABURNUM. The lovely Golden Rain is normally grown in gardens as a specimen standard, but it is, in fact, an edge of woodland plant and hence does well under taller things. A multiple-stemmed specimen on the north side of a great yew grows high enough to get its head in the sun and to make a marvellous display against the evergreen darkness. The Scotch Laburnum, *L. alpinum*, or one of its crosses with a common sort such as 'Vossii', have the longest racemes of flower. The golden-leaved form should be avoided on chalk soil: it looks just as if it were suffering from lime-induced chlorosis.

LAURUS nobilis *10 – 20 × 10ft (3 – 6 × 3m.)*
Sweet bay is not for cold areas but in most of maritime Britain (there are fine bushes, for instance, in Dundee) it makes a good plant. Where happy it flowers and seeds itself around, in deep shade. The narrow-leaved form, 'angustifolia', is reputedly hardier.

LAVANDULA. ADS Lavenders are generally for sun. But see the remarks under Cistus: again dry shade is accepted by many Mediterraneans.

LEYCESTERIA formosa.   *6 − 8 × 5ft (2 − 2·5 × 1·5m.)*
June–September

Himalayan Honeysuckle can be a striking plant with its pairs of leaves up green, white-bloomed stems and arching spikes of white flowers. The purple of their bracts is continued as the flowers are replaced by shining berries. It does best in moist soil and at least half shade when it will seed itself around.

LIGUSTRUM. Ordinary privet is one of the dullest plants, a reputation gained sadly because of its ability to put up with everything. It thus gets the dullest sites. But there is more to privet than this.

japonicum   *6 − 8 × 6ft (2 − 2·5 × 2m.)*   *August–September*

A good thick evergreen for half-shade hedge or screen-making. Its form 'Rotundifolium' is very slow-growing, making a tight, dark Bonsai-like specimen. It looks well in a Chinese pickled-cabbage jar in a shady paved court.

lucidum   *10 − 30 × 15ft (3 − 10 × 4·5m.)*   *September*

A lovely broad-leaved evergreen for year-round interest which lights itself up in early autumn with diffuse particles of white flowers. The variegated form is excellent and flowers almost as well.

ovalifolium   *8 − 10 × 8ft (2·5 − 3 × 2·5m.)*   *July*

The ubiquitous privet, whose two-coloured leaved variants are, unpruned, invaluable shrubs for shade. If light concentration is not too low the golden 'Aureum' is as bright from a distance as forsythia. Silver Privet, 'Argenteum', by comparison, has green leaves, white-edged. Both provide excellent cut foliage throughout the year.

97

LONICERA. In addition to the climbing honeysuckles the genus holds numbers of shrubs, several of which flower well enough in half shade to make a show, albeit a rather fleeting one. These include species such as *L. korolkowii* and *L. syringantha*. For our needs in shade the genus holds one outstanding plant. This is

pileata   *2 – 3 × 5ft (600 – 900mm. × 1·5m.)   June*

A semi-evergreen of almost *Cotoneaster horizontalis* shape, it is excellent in similar positions — for shady banks or under light trees. It has several particular moments of quiet attraction; in summer when a waft of typically honeysuckle fragrance comes from the little hidden flowers; in autumn when it is worth picking a few sprays for the transluscent purple berries; and in spring when the fresh leaves start to replace the old dark ones.

MAGNOLIA.
See page 59.

MAHONIA. One of the few absolutely invaluable genera for shade planting. It includes extremely choice species as well as those which are indestructibly easy. All are beautiful.

aquifolium   *3 × 3ft (1 × 1m.)   March–April*

Although planted by the acre for game coverts the Oregon Grape is still of great individual beauty. Whorls of burnished pinnate leaves are topped in spring by heads of bright yellow flowers which become grape-bloomed fruits in late summer and autumn. Some forms have leaves which turn red and purple in the autumn: it even succeeds under beeches and a clump or two can look lovely thus with just the right textural effect to contrast with the trees' elephant-grey smoothness.

Several good garden hybrids have some *aquifolium* blood (or sap). These include the smaller 'Moseri' and bigger 'Aldenhamensis'. *Pinnata* and *repens* are two other good species from western North America.

japonica   *6 × 8ft (2 × 2·5m.)   November–March*

This superb species only wants copious crops of delicious fruit to make it the ultimate desirable plant. Apart from this it really does have everything: magnificent evergreen leaves, long sprays of scented flowers carried throughout the dullest months of the year and a strikingly architectural habit. It looks equally well in the informality of woodland or in a sophisticated court-yard. It is utterly hardy.

Although now a common plant and used in quantity in landscapers' schemes it is still seen at its best as the dominant individual of a carefully composed association. (*M. bealei* is the less good shrub, with short vertical spikes of flower and broader leaves often nomenclaturally confused with it.)

lomariifolia   *8 – 10 × 3ft (2·5 – 3 × 1m.)*
November–December

A splendid shrub for woodland or the darkest corner of a sheltered courtyard. The long primate leaves are carried in whorls up the strongly vertical stems and each is topped with a great shuttlecock of deep yellow flowers. A floral exclamation to end each year with a bang.

x **media** is the name now given to a group of plants produced by various crosses of the two previously listed species. 'Charity', 'Buckland' and 'Winter Sun' are perhaps the best known of an increasing number. Each variously combines the differing attributes of the parents: in habit and flower colour they lean towards *M. lomariifolia* yet inherit hardiness from *M. japonica*. None have the length of flowering time nor the fragrance of the latter: God's is the better plant.

Mild gardens with plenty of room for a dramatic effect should try, if they can get them, further dramatic foliage plants such as *M. acanthifolia* and *M. napaulensis*.

MALUS. This is not the place for a discourse on the ornamental apples: many indeed are big enough to be shade providers rather than taking on the subordinate role of being plants for shade. Yet it is worth remembering that our native Crab Apple *M. sylvestris* (literally 'of the woods') is a hedgerow and woodland plant, as are most of its relatives around the world. Thus they succeed admirably in the light shade of open woodland. This causes rather more open growth and less flower, giving a lighter and, in many ways, more beautiful effect than the solid lumps of unadulterated colour, however magnificent, of specimen lawn trees.

OSMANTHUS. Several good evergreen shrubs with highly fragrant small white flowers are happy in at least half shade.

delavayi   *6 × 6ft (2 × 2m.)*   *April*

The best known of the genus. A tidy, slow-growing plant, covering itself with white in its season.

x **Osmarea burkwoodii**, a putative bigeneric hybrid with *Phillyrea decora*, is rather similar with longer leaves and a more robust habit.

x **fortunei**   *10 × 8ft (3 × 2·5m.)*   *September–November*

The highly scented *O. fragrans* met with in mediterranean gardens and those in south-east United States is not safe here. But this hybrid, of which *O. fragrans* is a parent, is only marginally less delicious. The general effect is that of a broad-leaved holly.

heterophyllus   *8 – 10 × 8ft (2·5 – 3 × 2·5m.)*   *October*

The type is a slow-growing rather dull shrub but its variegated forms can be very attractive. Leaves are rather like those of a small holly and extremely variable in shape: on the same branch they may be broad and spined or narrow and smooth. Young growth emerges attractively purple-tinged.

PHILADELPHUS. The lovely mock-oranges are not for deepest shade (although *P. coronarius* will grow even under holm-oaks it flowers there rather poorly so there is not much point) but, like Deutzias to which they are related, half shade from above and north-facing borders are perfectly acceptable. In such positions the somewhat short flowering season is extended, especially in a hot June. They should be planted where the drifts of perfume can be appreciated on midsummer evenings.

coronarius ADS   *8 − 10 × 8ft (2·5 − 3 × 2·5m.)   June*

However common, this is a beautiful plant when covered with its creamy fragrant flowers. It has a good variegated form and a superlative gold-leaved one, which flowers as well as the type. This plant really does need shade, especially in the south, otherwise the young growth scorches in full sun.

Hybridization has produced some excellent garden plants. Several are really small, only 3ft (1m.) high or so, such as 'Manteau d'Hermine' and 'Avalanche'. Bigger, around 5ft (1·5m.) high, are those incorporating the rather tender Mexican, *P. maculatus*. These have inherited a purple patch at the base of their petals: particularly good are 'Beauclerk' and 'Belle Étoile'.

PHILLYREA. ADS A small group of Mediterranean evergreens which can take tree shade until they themselves become of small tree size.

P. latifolia has been confused with the olive (which is greyer in leaf and blows silver in the wind) because of its showering habit. A beautiful plant when mature.

POTENTILLA. The shrubby cinquefoils flower best in full sun but in a north-facing border they still put on a sufficient show to make themselves worthwhile. They are very late to come into leaf (one is always convinced that new plantings are dead) so are a good shrub layer above early bulbs in a small stratified association.

arbuscula   *1½ × 3ft (450 × 900mm.)   July–October*

Big yellow flowers for a long period on a dwarf bush: this is a good front-of-border plant.

fruticosa   *3 – 4 × 4ft (1 – 1·2 × 1·2m.)   May–October*

This has produced a large number of forms varying in leaf colour from white ('Beanii') through all shades of yellow to orange ('Tangerine') and now vermilion ('Red Ace'). Particularly good is 'Elizabeth', product of a cross between the two species listed here.

PRUNUS. Of the flowering cherries much the same can be said as of Malus but in addition the evergreen cherry laurels provide excellent shade plants under trees or even in really dark town gardens. Here their lustrous leaves pick up and reflect all available light. It will be recalled also that Morello cherries were a classic north-wall plant of grand kitchen gardens. There is no reason why its spring flowers and summer fruits should not be enjoyed in humbler (and more convenient) positions in gardens of today.

laurocerasus   *15 – 20 × 20ft (4·5 – 6 × 6m.)   April*

A superb plant in all its parts. Leaves can be as fine as many rhododendrons and much more shining; white flowers in long spikes make a distinctive show and in good years the ripening cherries make a fine autumn display (they are delicious if you can beat the birds to them). There are several variations in size and shape. Two invaluable dwarfs are 'Otto Luykens' and 'Zabeliana'.

Cherry laurel is not for exposed positions over chalk but in alkaline woodland with a good humus layer it is fine. Better in thin chalk soils is

lusitanica   *15 − 20 × 15ft (4·5 − 6 × 4·5m.)*

The Portugal Laurel is smaller in scale, a useful tidy evergreen.
The long spikes of white flowers appear in June often in great
profusion. 'Variegata' is a good striped form.

PYRACANTHA. There are few plants which put on such a
double show as the firethorns. The narrow evergreen leaves
disappear once in June under clouds of hawthorn-like flower
and again, in good years, under berries in autumn. Again, as
with Cotoneaster (near relations) the scarlet-fruited forms can
be stripped by birds in a few days: where this is likely, orange
and yellow types maintain their display much longer.

All make admirable north-wall plants and trained espalier
fashion can create a fine formal effect. Amongst the best are

atalantioides   *10 − 15 × 10ft (3 − 4·5 × 3m.)   May–June*

A fine Chinese species whose red berries usually last well.
'Aurea' has yellow fruit.

coccinea 'Lalandei'   *10 − 15 × 10ft (3 − 4·5 × 3m.)   June*

A vigorous shrub with relatively broad leaves and masses of
orange-red fruits. 'Orange Glow' is a hybrid, making an
impenetrable mass of thorny shoots and carrying long-lasting
crops of fruit.

RHAMNUS. This group of generally unexciting shrubs contains
several with medicinal properties, including the producer of
cascara sagrada. Ornamentally, for shaded borders, even under
trees the variegated form of *R. alaterna* is worth searching out:
it makes a 10-foot high evergreen whose leaves are attractively
marbled with grey and cream.

RIBES. There are few more spectacular north-wall plants than
well-fruited, cordon-trained red and white currants: unfortunately to satisfy the stomach one has to deprive the eye.

Ornamentally the flowering currants of North America and the Orient are excellent shade-tolerant shrubs.

laurifolium   *2 × 3ft (600 × 900mm.)   February–March*

An evergreen with corrugated leaves and a good display of pale green flowers in late winter. It builds up a lovely group in shade with *Helleborus corsicus* and the later snowdrops.

odoratum   *5 × 4ft (1·5 × 1·2m.)   April*

Good golden spikes of flower, scented of cloves. X *gordonianum*, its hybrid with the next species, is extraordinarily intermediate in type with highly original orange-bronze flowers.

sanguineum   *6 × 5ft (2 × 1·5m.)   March–April*

The lovely pink-flowering currant, an almost inevitable associate of Forsythia, is said by its detractors to have a feline fragrance (though they seldom describe it so delicately): certainly it is distinctive, although not necessarily unpleasant. Flower colour variants extend from white to deep red ('Pulborough Scarlet'). All are happy in half shade, and for the dwarf golden-leaved form 'Brocklebankii' it is essential.

ROSA. Although some rose species grow well enough in shade their flowering and fruiting are restricted. Obviously therefore no general recommendation can be given. But there are at least two exceptions. The lovely little Scotch Burnet Roses (*R. spinosissima*) will make their low thickets in dry shade and, because any reduction of flowers and hips is not important, *R. rubrifolia* is still invaluable. Its elegant shape and grey-purple stems and leaves combine perfectly with martagon lilies or, later, with pink Japanese anemones. Modern bush roses so grown become etiolated and weak. But a few climbers (q.v.) are admirable north-wall plants.

RUBUS. Our own blackberry perfectly demonstrates the process of succession in woodland regeneration. It quickly moves in to an open glade to take over from herbaceous things but is eventually shaded out by the trees to which it gave protection while they were still seedlings. A few exotic brambles can take more shade.

cockburnianus   *6 − 8 × 6ft (2 − 2·5 × 2m.)   June*

For a dark spot, though not in tree drip, this 'whitewash bramble' creates a splendid winter eye-catcher with its fountain of vivid white stems. Flower and fruit are pretty undistinguished and the old stems are best cut out to allow full development of the new. *R. biflorus* is similar.

odoratus   *6 × 3ft (2 × 1m.)   June–September*

Good suckering ground-cover in open woodland or for a big north border. Rose-like flowers are followed by edible berries. There is a white form.

tricolor *2ft (600mm.) × infinity*

Excellent ground-cover. Long, red-bristled shoots with bright green leaves root as they go.

x **tridel**   *8 × 8ft (2·5 × 2·5m.)   May–June*

The big white dog-rose flowers line the branches of this fine open bush. Not for dense shade.

RUSCUS aculeatus ADS is Butcher's Broom, an odd, clump-forming spiny evergreen related, surprisingly, to the lilies. Flowers are insignificant and carried, apparently, in the centre of each leaf — but these must be botanically explained as cladodes, flattened stems. If both sexes are present the female has fine marble-sized bright scarlet berries: these used to be hawked round by gypsies for Christmas decorations. An hermaphrodite form exists and should be sought out. About 2 feet high.

hypoglossum ADS is a smaller plant with much bigger cladodes, and again accepts driest shade but seems not to grow with the freedom it does in warmer climates. It comes from southern Europe.

SAMBUCUS ADS. The elders are undervalued shrubs: accepting almost any conditions they are ideal woodland-edge plants.

canadensis *8 × 8ft (2·5 × 2·5m.) July*

The American Elder is best in its 'Maxima' form, pruned in spring like buddleia. Splendid divided foliage and huge flat flower heads result, followed by black berries.

nigra *10 – 15 × 10ft (3 – 4·5 × 3m.) June–July*

The most spectacular wildling of our chalkland hedgerows and eminently suitable for bringing into all but the most sophisticated gardens. The fragrant flower heads make wine (as do the purple berries) and that most delectable of country brews, elderflower champagne, which, fit to be drunk in a fortnight, is ideal for the impatient. Various forms exist with variegated, cut-leaved and golden leaves.

racemosa *8 – 10 × 8ft (2·5 – 3 × 2·5m.) April*

Here the greenish flower heads precede the foliage and are succeeded by bright red fruits ripening in summer at the same time as the rowan (one sometimes sees them together in Scottish woodland edges). Its form 'Plumosa Aurea', with golden fern-like foliage, is one of the best of foliage shrubs.

SARCOCOCCA ADS. Low box-like evergreens with highly scented petal-less flowers in winter followed by black berries. Happy under trees, although rather slow-growing.

confusa *2 × 3ft (600 × 900mm.) January–February*

A good tight little plant. Another species very similar is *ruscifolia chinensis*. The fruiting display can be good in December.

hookerana digyna   *2 × 2ft (600 × 600mm.)*
January–February

Longer, narrower leaves make this a more elegant plant, equally useful as evergreen hummocks to associate with the earliest spring bulbs under trees.

SKIMMIA. For small gardens as well as big here are some of the best shade-bearing shrubs. They are all low-growing dioecious evergreens with aromatic leaves. Only *S. reevesiana* is hermaphrodite and that, sadly, is calcicole.

japonica   *2 × 3ft (600 × 900mm.)*   *April*

Careful choice of the best forms provides leaf beauty throughout the year and a combination of flower and fruit for at least half of it. 'Foremanii' is the most vigorous of the females, with fine red berries held from late summer until the opening of next year's flowers. It ought to be planted in a 3:1 ratio with the male form 'Fragrans' or 'Rubella'. In both the scented flowers are in white heads but as a bonus the last named produces these as red buds as early as November, holding them thus until the following spring.

laureola   *2 × 3ft (600 × 900mm.)*   *April*

A good green-garden plant with its long lustrous leaves and heads of green-white flowers. The male form is most usually available.

SPIRAEA. A highly diverse genus with many good garden shrubs for spring and summer display. One or two of the commoner sorts, such as *S. salicifolia*, accept under-tree shade and make pleasant thickets in a wild place. Others are suitable for north-facing borders but resent tree drip.

x **bumalda** 'Anthony Waterer'   *3 × 2ft (900 ×600mm.)*
June–September

One of the best-loved front of border shrubs, it can be left shrubby or cut to the ground every spring. The current year's shoots carry flat heads of deep pink. 'Gold Flame' is a fine new selection with developing foliage of soft pinkish orange.

x **vanhouttei**   *5 × 5ft (1·5 × 1·5m.)   June*

An elegant shrub making a fountain of branches which foam with white flowers in their season.

STAPHYLEA. The Bladder Nuts are tall pale shrubs — the name referring to the inflated, poppable, seed capsules.

colchica 'Coulombieri'   *10 − 12 × 10ft (3 − 4 × 3m.)   May*

As the soft green leaves unfold, from the end of every twig a raceme of white gently scented flowers develops. This is a perfect plant for a half-shaded corner in a white garden.

holocarpa 'Rosea'   *8 − 10 × 10ft (2·5 − 3 × 3m.)   April–May*

A most distinct bladder nut with pale pink flower heads strung from the branches whose unfolding foliage is a complementary soft bronze.

STRANSVAESIA davidiana   *10 − 12 × 10ft (3 − 4 × 3m.)*

Like a lustrous cotoneaster (to which it is related) this splendid distinct evergreen has white flowers and brilliant autumn fruits. These are enhanced by a random selection of the older leaves attempting to match them in colour. There is a yellow-fruited form as well as one which remains prostrate.

SYMPHORICARPUS ADS. The snowberries make pleasant thickets of twiggy growth, unexciting in flower but with pleasant grey-green leaves and grape-sized berries making a long-lasting autumn show.

rivularis   *5 × 5ft (1·5 × 1·5m.)   June*

This is the commonest snowberry, often planted as game covert and hence perfectly happy under trees. *S. albus* is similar but smaller. Hybrids now include 'Magic Berry' and 'Mother of Pearl', with rose pink berries in such quantity that the branches are bowed down with their weight. 'White Hedge' and 'Erect' are more upright and can be used as small internal hedges in shade: the latter has pink fruit. Birds generally leave them alone.

VIBURNUM. Many species of this lovely genus are invaluable in shaded spots for either flower or fruit (but seldom, it must be admitted, for both).

For Fruit

betulifolium   *12 × 10ft (4 × 3m.)   June*

A vigorous plant which wants a lot of room, especially as three or so are needed to ensure pollination. Such a group when mature and arched over with copious crops of vivid shining berries is a remarkable sight.

davidii   *2 × 4ft (600mm. × 1·2m.)   June*

Grown more for its evergreen foliage and generally tidy, ground-hugging habit, an inter-pollinating group does produce fruit of unusual colour — clear turquoise blue. A most valuable plant.

x hillieri   *8 × 8ft (2·5 × 2·5m.)   June*

A strong evergreen hybrid, one of many fine Hillier plants. It lays claim to being as dual-purpose a Viburnum as any, with cream flowers in June and good crops of red berries turning to black. Foliage is always of interest.

opulus   *10 × 10ft (3 × 3m.)   July*

One of our most beautiful native woodlanders. Its flat white flower heads are like those of lace-cap hydrangeas, with a circlet of ray florets (and, like hydrangeas, there is a sterile 'mop-head' form, the well-known Guelder Rose). The species also has fine crops of brilliant red-currant fruits: a couple of good yellow-fruited forms are also available.

Flowering Viburnums.

Most of these are happy in half-shade and have pink-flushed white flowers, highly scented.

x bodnantense   *8 − 10 × 6ft (2·5 − 3 × 2m.)   November–March*

One of the very best of winter-flowering plants and much more effective in shade than its *farreri* (*fragrans*) parent. During the summer its thick purple-flushed leaves create a sombre note but as they gently turn colour and fall the first flowers open, small heads of apple-blossom colour, heavily scented. The display continues off and on for three months, being hardly affected by frost: a most comforting plant.

carlesii   *4 − 5 × 5ft (1·2 − 1·5 × 1·5m.)   April*

This lovely plant is well-known. It appreciates shade from the east to reduce damage from late spring frost, to which it is subject, and the half-shade extends the rather short flowering season.

This is extended well in some of its hybrid offspring. x *burkwoodii* starts to flower soon after Christmas, lasting till May and is semi-evergreen: its rather lank growth makes it a good wall-plant, even facing north. *V.* x *juddii* and 'Anne Russell' hark back more to *carlesii* itself but are often better 'doers' than the parent and with a more extended season.

plicatum   *6 × 6ft (2 × 2m.)   May–June*

Like Staphylea, in flower the Japanese Snowball is a marvellously 'cool' plant. Round heads of sterile flowers are brightly
green to begin with and gradually whiten. The bigger 'Grandiflorum' is the one to grow. These were popular garden plants in
the Orient long before they were introduced to Britain by
Robert Fortune in the 1840s. The wild type which followed
later, as with our own Snowball Tree, has flower heads with just
one outside ring of big sterile florets. Its garden effect, however, is made dramatic by the wide-tiered branch pattern upon
which the flower clusters stand like a field of filigree mushrooms. The best forms are 'Lanarth', 'Rowallane' (this often
fruits well, too) and 'Pink Beauty'. All these Japanese Snow-
balls appreciate woodland half-shade and a leafy moist soil, but
have no objection to lime in it.

rhytidophyllum ADS   *12 × 10ft (4 × 3m.)   May*

Although quite striking in flower and, in a good year (if planted
with others) in fruit, it is as a foliage plant that this is particularly
grown. It seems to raise strong feelings, being loved or loathed,
with little in between. This may be related to the site in which it
is seen. Though 'ADS', the great corrugated leaves pick up and
hold dust and give an air of summer exhaustion. In a clean,
country site, planted to build up an architectural effect with
Fatsia, for example, it can look dramatic.

tinus ADS   *8 – 10 × 10ft (2·5 – 3× 3m.)   January–April*

Laurustinus is one of the very best of evergreen shrubs. Remarkably hardy for a Mediterranean, its white flowers are set off
against lustrous leaves throughout the darkest months. Several
good forms have been selected: those with bigger leaves such as
lucidum, and 'Variegatum' are rather less hardy but the compact, pale pink flowered 'Eve Price' is as safe as the type. This is
the one for small gardens. If pollination is successful the
autumn fruiting effect is also good: metallic blue turning black.

Laurustinus is sufficiently formal for courtyard use — it accepts trimming happily, yet is free enough for the open garden. A most adaptable plant.

VINCA. Periwinkles are amongst the most valuable ground cover shrubs for shade. On banks, difficult otherwise to maintain, they form a perfect layer of foliage and they are equally at home under shrubs and trees.

major. Greater Periwinkle is so strong a grower with its long, arching shoots rooting at the tips, that in small gardens it may need to be contained. Nonetheless even here, the variegated form in particular — which has clear blue flowers like the type — is excellent to put in a narrow bed under north-facing windows or used in a clipped circle under a specimen lawn tree where grass fails.

minor. Lesser Periwinkle, though smaller in leaf and flower is no less vigorous and is quite capable of climbing into and over small shrubs, as does Lamiastrum (q.v., herbaceous list). Under big mature shrubs all is well and charming variants from the normal blue exist with purple or white flowers, single and double as well as those with yellow and white variegated leaves.

WEIGELA. Sprays of foxglove-like flowers in May and June on easily grown shrubs make this a useful group. Not for densest shade, which causes etiolation and lack of flower but in north-facing mixed shrub borders they do well. Hybrids based upon *W. florida* are produced mainly in shades of pink and red (though 'Mont Blanc' is a good white). But perhaps the most desirable of all is *W.f.* 'Variegata'. Here the soft pink flowers open with the pink tinged cream and green young leaves and combine together in an entirely beautiful way. If the older flowered shoots are then cut away further strong variegated shoots develop to maintain the foliage effect till autumn.

7 Plants for Shady Walls

It has already been mentioned more than once that walls in shade offer marvellous potential to the adventurous gardener. If shelter as well as shade is also provided,a wide range of plants, otherwise frost-tender, becomes possible: only east walls liable to the effects of early morning sun must be treated with care. North walls, surprisingly, are often far preferable. Walled town gardens and courtyards can be turned into exotic bowers of lushest growth: the intention as with open-ground borders should be to create a combination of colours and textures from flower and foliage to give interest throughout the year. Formality is introduced by rigorously trained fruit trees or pyracanthas; its opposite by an apparently uncontrived and uncontrolled association of plants big and small.

Effective support is vital for there are very few self-clinging ornamentals (perhaps, when one thinks of the vigour of Virginia Creeper, or Boston Ivy, this is just as well). Many wall-plants are twiners, such as honeysuckle and wisteria: these need vertical supports. Others have adaptations of leaf, stem or stipule which grow into tendrils. Clematis has twisting petioles. All these can hold onto horizontal support. Thus, to cater for all tastes and to achieve relative permanence walls are best given tightly strained wide-meshed pig or sheep wire. Knocking in nails and twiddling a bit of string ahead of plant growth is doomed to disaster, sooner or later and usually the former.

In addition to plants directly adapted to climbing in one way or another and hence needing support, numbers of good plants such as camellias already mentioned in the general list can use a wall at their back with advantage and may indeed demand it in cold areas.

One further point should be mentioned. Most plants climb in order to get a place in the sun. Ivy is a classic example; not only does it not flower until it has reached the top of its chosen support — tree or building — but having got there it celebrates the occasion by changing entirely its leaf shape and growth pattern. Thus most shady wall plants flower most at the top, some hardly at all until they flop over to the sunny side. This is particularly galling if this is to next door, and one's neighbours, however loved, get all the benefit. Again therefore very dark spots, vertical as well as horizontal, will be enlivened not by a blaze of flower colour but by diversity of foliage. In the following list this is emphasised.

ACTINIDIA chinensis. This is the Chinese Gooseberry or Kiwi Fruit (the first name reflects its country of origin, the second where it has been most exploited: neither name its botanical relationship). Here, especially in half-shade it seldom fruits much even if a pollinator is provided, but the hairy stems and big leaves make a fine pattern.

AKEBIA quinata. Five-lobed leaves, softly plum-purple as they unfold, are accompanied by hanging clusters of fleshy flowers of a similar colour. Occasionally the colour is repeated yet again by edible fruit the shape of small mangoes. Not a dramatic plant yet it always causes interest. Other members of its rather esoteric family *Lardizabalaceae* if ever offered in a nursery list, should be tried. They include Stauntonia, Holboellia and the type-genus, Lardizabala, itself.

ARISTOLOCHIA macrophylla. A twiner which will get high if there is space but can be contained. The big smooth heart-shaped leaves make a strong effect.

BERBERIDOPSIS corallina. A lovely Chilean evergreen which really needs shade. It likes a lime-free soil and a sheltered wall where it will drape itself with drooping clusters of dark red flowers whose shape gives the plant its name.

CLEMATIS. Both the big-flowered hybrids and the species are apt to behave in the classic shady wall-plant way — growing like fun but flowering little until they get into the sun at the top. This behaviour should be worked with, rather than against. Clematis enjoy shade at the root as much as they enjoy sun at the head, hence the less rampant ones are admirable for growing through and up other things whose season of flowering they can either complement or extend by their own at another time. Of the numerous big-flowered hybrids, those with pale flowers such as the lovely and ubiquitous 'Nelly Moser' are actually best against north walls where the petals do not scorch. The choice here is wide and specialist catalogues (and Mr Christopher Lloyd's book on the genus) should be consulted.

alpina. A delicate species ideal for just this use. Flowering in late spring, it is ideal for putting up a climbing rose. 'Frances Rivis' is the best form, with blue and white flowers and silky seed-heads to follow. *C. macropetala* is rather similar, flowering later. It looks well with the old 'Crimson Glory' rose.

chrysocoma. For a wall which has not the space for the better known *montana* this pale pink charmer is ideal. Flowering begins in May and continues off and on for weeks.

cirrhosa. A sheltered half-shaded west wall offers a suitable site for an uncommon but very worthwhile species. In its Mediterranean home, scrambling up amongst the evergreen shrubs of the maquis, its flowers, cream coloured and cowslip scented, appear at Christmas, with us a little later.

montana. This vigorous climber is one of the joys of the late spring scene, romping over trees or up high walls. It accepts shade happily but when trained on a wall care must be given to leading young shoots (like geese, they will not be driven) where they are required: once the leaf-petioles have wrapped themselves round any support nothing can change their habit. The typical form is white: 'Rubens' and 'Tetrarose' are pink.

tangutica. Not for dark spots but in dappled shade this makes a tangle of shoots. From August the nodding yellow flowers, like myriad Tiffany lamps, hang out from the leaves. Early flowers are quickly succeeded by fluffy seed-heads and the mixed display continues until the first frosts.

GARRYA elliptica. Not a climber, but a robust and well-known open-ground evergreen shrub grown, in its male form, for the winter flowers. These are in the form of long grey-green catkins which in detail are identical with the husk and dart decoration so commonly used in late eighteenth-century plasterwork: as the plant was not introduced to western Europe until 1821 and the Adam brothers could not have seen it, this must be considered another example of Wilde's presumption of nature imitating art. Theories of aesthetics apart, Garrya is particularly ornamental as a wall, even a north-wall, plant, when the elegant tassels can reach 9 in (230 mm) or more in length. As a Californian it seems to resent cold draughts and even in the south Cotswolds, for example, leaves of exposed plants become scorched and unsightly.

HEDERA There is no genus more valuable to the shade-gardener. As ground cover, pot-plant and self-clinging wall-covering the lustrous leaves always appear fresh and tidy. Small- or large-leaved forms are available to suit any scale of planting. For dark walls the brighter variegated forms such as the big 'Paddy's Pride' and the smaller 'Gold Heart' are ideal. For ground cover the big-leaved 'Hibernica' is possibly the best.

HUMULUS lupulus. For putting the bitter into beer, the hop has no equal. As a rapid *herbaceous* climber it is also of use. Unfortunately the golden-leaved form reverts to green in full shade.

HYDRANGEA petiolaris is one of the very best climbers for a shady wall of any aspect. When growing well it is self-clinging. The white lace-cap flower heads expand in June and look well even in decline.

If they can be found, other climbing Hydrangeas are equally

deserving of space: these include *Schizophragma*, *Decumaria* and the evergreen *Pileostegia viburnoides*: all are eye-catching plants, but often slow to get going.

JASMINUM nudiflorum. It is fortunate that the best hardy winter-flowering Jasmine is entirely happy on a shady wall. Few garden pleasures are greater in the dark winter months than to be able to pick, again and again, sprays of yellow stars for an indoor vase. It is not a natural climber and needs care and encouragement if good wall-covering is to be maintained.

LAPAGERIA rosea. This delicious exotic aptly commemorates the Empress Josephine, whose maiden name was de la Pagerie. A Chilean (in fact that country's national flower) it needs a sheltered, shaded and lime-free spot and thus is not for all hands. But where it succeeds it is an annual autumnal surprise. From wiry twining shoots hang long narrow lily-like flowers of a thick waxy texture, bright rose red. Lapageria climbing through a camellia produces an extraordinary effect of a decorated Christmas tree, with both decoration and tree exaggerated to a point near absurdity. But very beautiful.

LONICERA. As a plant of our own woodlands, the common honeysuckle is unsurpassed for scenting a shady wall. Few plants are more evocative of the perfect cottage garden and few easier to grow — so long as a virulent aphis is controlled. 'Early Dutch' and 'Late Dutch' are often offered as selections: together they combine to give a June to October flowering period.

japonica halliana. Equally fragrant, this evergreen species bears its smaller cream-coloured flowers in the axils of its young shoots. Lovely sprays can be cut for the house from June to Christmas. It is very vigorous and training should try to avoid too great a tangle building up. If it does, the brave gardener cuts it to the ground in spring: it will usually recover.

A variegated form with elegant gold-netted leaves makes good ground cover but very seldom flowers.

tragophylla. This is visually a lovely climber, revelling in full shade, with long deep-yellow flowers. But honeysuckles ought to be scented and this is not. *L.* x. *tellmanniana*, a hybrid of it, is equally beautiful and equally flawed. Perhaps one expects too much.

PARTHENOCISSUS. The brilliant autumn colours expected of Virginia Creeper and Boston Ivy are naturally muted in shade, yet they grow no less well and are unsurpassed for providing a self-clinging cover to the highest wall (until, that is, tower blocks became an urban architectural cliché). These are respectively the American *P. quinquefolia* and the Japanese *P. tricuspidata* 'Veitchii'.

henryana. A less robust plant and very good for a shady courtyard, where the bands of silver on the leaves become particularly marked.

POLYGONUM baldschuanicum. The well-known Russian Vine, growing up through the branches of, say, a full-grown yew and foaming with flower like a shaken magnum of champagne, is a magnificent sight. But it is not a plant for a small garden, except for non-gardeners, who may put in a single plant and then sit back, well back.

SCHIZANDRA is a small genus of Oriental twiners, with flowers somewhat similar to Berberidopsis. Any that are available are likely to succeed on shaded sheltered walls.

TRACHELOSPERMUM. Although always recommended as plants for sunny walls they will in fact flower well in shade in a sheltered position — a south wall under summer-tree shade, for instance. Rather jasmine-like, the cream-coloured rotate corollas are heavily fragrant. *T. asiaticum* is the hardiest species but *T. jasminoides* is pretty safe in the south and west.

VITIS. The true vines, grown either for grapes or for autumn colour are not plants for shade, but *V. coignetiae* is a worthy candidate because, although its normally dramatic autumn tints are toned down out of the sun, the huge heart-shaped leaves create a fine effect in their own right. It can be as rampant as Russian Vine but carefully pruned in winter to a spur system and pinched back in summer it can be contained even in a small courtyard. The subsequent effect is worth the trouble.

8 Herbaceous Plants for Shade

ACANTHUS. It might seem perverse to begin this list with a plant whose name and use as the inspiration for the carved capitals of classical Corinthian columns epitomizes hot Mediterranean hillsides in a blaze of full sun. Yet paradoxically they will grow in at least half-shade: flowering will be less good but their splendid clumps of leaves, as architectural in growth as are their idealized shapes beneath a pediment, are just as good. As discussed in detail with the Cistuses, here is a southern European which is used to rock-shades, olive groves or the maquis and hence with us accepts dry shade remarkably well.

mollis ADS   *2 × 3ft (600 × 900mm.) (flower spikes 4 − 5ft (1·2 × 1·5m.) high)*

The plant generally available, and in fact the best, is *A.m. latifolius*, with great arching leaves. These are so bright and shiny that they pick up flecks of dappled shade and flash it back, and it is one of the few plants to give a dry spot an entirely false air of moist lushness.

spinosus ADS   *2 × 2ft (600 × 600mm.)*

A smaller plant but still of great presence and which flowers more consistently. The flowers are individually rather foxglove-like, in strong spiny spikes. Picked and dried when newly out they are admirable for winter decoration indoors.

ACONITUM. These are the Monkshoods which, in shade and generally less sophisticated areas of the garden than formal herbaceous borders, satisfactorily take the place of their delphinium relations. Blues or purples are typical colours in tall spikes above elegantly fingered leaves. The roots possess a poison to which there is no known antidote, but as no one is likely to eat them this dread fact need not put off even the most nervous.

napellus *4 – 5 × 1ft (1·2 – 1·5m. × 300mm.)*
August–September

This is the common European Monkshood, cultivated here since the sixteenth century. It is one of those good herbaceous plants that with little help can maintain itself in the shady rough turf of old orchards and help to carry on a flowering meadow feeling long after the spring bulbs are over. The soft pink form 'Carneum' does particularly well in northern and Scottish gardens.

variegatum *5 × 2ft (1·5m. × 600mm.)   August–September*

Where the Common Monkshood has straight unbranched spikes this species holds its paler helmets on elegant branching stems.

Both of these species have been used by breeders to provide a fine range of hybrids of varying colours. They appear in nurserymen's lists under *A.* x *bicolor* plus a cultivar name. The older types are tall elegant plants for big borders or half-wild places while the newer Bressingham varieties are typically shorter and sturdier.

vulparia *4 – 5 × 1ft (1·2 – 1·5m. × 300mm.)   July–August*

Here is a yellow species, a sort of horn yellow, on a lax elegant-leaved plant. Reputedly, its root-poison is sufficient to have caused its use as a vermin-killer and hence the common name of Wolf's-bane.

ACORUS calamus *2 × 1ft (600 × 300mm.)*

The striped variegated form of this pleasant iris-like waterside plant is suitable for damp shade in association with primulas, contrasting its vertical emphasis with the broader leaves of hostas. A member of the arum family, it lacks a spathe and hence the flowers make no effect. An alternative virtue lies in the aromatic scent from the crushed leaves, which give its vernacular name — 'Sweet Flag'.

ACTAEA. A small group of odd plants, quietly beautiful in leaf, flower and, surprisingly for herbaceous plants, in fruit. The leaves are dissected and rather fern-like, and above these are held the fuzzy flower heads reminiscent of thalictrums (meadow-rues) to which Actaea is related. The berries are very poisonous. The three species grown all enjoy shade and a leafy soil.

alba   *2½ × 1½ft (760 × 450mm.)*

Although the name applies to the flower colour it really refers to the glistening white berries, each one enhanced by the swollen scarlet stalk with which it is attached to the spike. This is a real eye-stopper in August, planted in an area devoted to spring bulbs which at this time are out of sight.

rubra   *2½ × 1½ft (760 × 450mm)*

Here the heads of berries, as bright as clustered redcurrants, become spectacular in September. While the plant flourishes in full shade, a gleam of sun at some time of the day enhances its effect, which is good for a couple of months.

spicata   *1½ × 1½ft (450 × 450mm.)*

Unlike the above two species which are native to North America (and collected early: John Tradescant knew the former in the early seventeenth century), this is the rare Herb Christopher of our own northern woods. Smaller, but no less eye-catching, the berries are as shining black as those of true Deadly Nightshade — and equally not to be eaten.

AJUGA reptans   *9in × 12in (25 × 300mm.)   April–May*

The Bugle of moist woodland rides makes good front-of-bed growth, with leaves nearly flat on the ground and pleasant spikes of dark blue flowers. There are purple-leaved and multi-coloured-leaved forms which need sun to colour and are rather pointless in shade, but the charming little 'Variegata', whose leaves are splashed with white and grey, thrives.

ALCHEMILLA. The Lady's Mantles are elegantly leaved plants of woodland edges and upland pastures. Even the smallest or most ordinary are worth growing but in the context of this list *A. mollis* from Asia Minor is supreme. While it takes full sun in a moist soil (and in the north) it seems particularly right in at least half shade. The pleated silky leaves are of the softest grey-green, and above them the light heads of gold-green flowers are held for weeks in early summer. Eighteen inches (450mm.) high.

It makes a lovely edging to a shady path and will seed itself about under shrubs and in the interstices of informal paving, and always looks well. Seldom does it outstay its welcome; dead-heading before the seeds are shed will obviously reduce its spread. Usually, however, the seedlings are appreciated in someone else's garden as soon as one's own reaches satiety.

ANAPHALIS. If one thinks about it there are very few grey-leaved plants for shade. The reasons are clear enough: the hairy felting which usually gives the effect is a xeromorphic adaptation to protect the plant from excess sun or drying winds. Neither is a problem in woodland. Thus one is both surprised and grateful for the following pair of Himalayans which are invaluable in shady borders.

cinnamomea   *2 × 2ft (600 × 600mm.)   August–September*

This is more usually seen in the lists as *A. (Gnaphthalium) yedoense*. It has white under-leaves and felted stalks which carry flat heads of white everlasting flowers. Their papery consistency naturally enables them to last well.

triplinervis   *1 × 2ft (300 × 600mm.)   July–September*

A shorter plant and perhaps even more desirable for providing the texture and colour of grey Mediterraneans in a shady spot, though not for dry shade.

ANEMONE. The windflowers offer many lovely plants for our needs, from little woodland carpeters, epitomized by our own Wood Anemone, to robust herbaceous plants. All, regardless of size, are elegant and light in effect.

x **hybrida**   *4 − 5 × 2ft (1·2 − 1·5m. × 600mm.)   August–October*

It is simpler, if botanically inexact, to put under this name all the so-called Japanese Anemones (*A. japonica, A. hupehensis*). They are easy, common, plants and often rather invasive but provide with little effort on the part of the grower some of the loveliest sights of the garden year.

The fine dark leaves are shaped more like several plants (e.g. Abutilon) with a *vitifolia* epithet than vine itself, and through them push the tall, near leafless, flower stems. The flowers are like flat single roses, white, pale or dark pink, each with a fine central boss of yellow stamens. Several named cultivars are offered. They associate particularly well in a north-facing herbaceous border with the anaphalises described above.

nemorosa   *6 × 6in. (150 × 150mm.)*

The exquisite windflower or wood anemone of our deciduous woodlands can hardly be seen to better advantage than in its natural habitat of russet-coloured tree-leaf-litter, primroses and fresh spears of bluebell leaves. This tells us how they are ideally used but they succeed equally under shrubs and even in weak orchard grass. The normal type is white, often pinkish in bud, but some fine selected forms are available. 'Allenii' is the biggest and best of the blues.

Other anemones to search out and use in shade are *Aa. narcissiflora, rivularis, sylvestris.*

ANEMONOPSIS

macrophylla   *2½ × 1½ft (760 × 460mm.)   July*

This is one of the plants which make any plantsman long for the ideal, deep, leafy-soil woodland. Yet the north border or the shady raised bed make equally good homes for the fern-like leaves and nodding purple flowers.

ANGELICA archangelica   *5 × 3ft (1·5 × 1m.)   June–July*

The great spherical umbels of green flowers above cool green leaves amply embody Marvell's line 'a green thought in a green shade'. As a statuesque clump in isolation or towering above hostas and smilacina the effect is splendid. But it is biennial and replacements must be kept to hand. Fortunately Angelica seeds itself about and any excess can be candied to remind ourselves that many of those green strips on cakes today are plastic.

AQUILEGIA. Most of the modern hybrid long-spurred columbines of North American origin do best in sun but our own native Granny's Bonnet is a woodlander and enjoys conditions provided by garden shade so long as moisture is adequate.

vulgaris   *3 × 1½ft (1m. × 460mm.)*

seeds itself around in a range of colours, blue, purple, pink and white above its elegant glaucous leaves. Smaller, with *A. alpina* as its other parent, is the hybrid 'Hensol Harebell', 2½ × 1ft (760 × 300mm.), which also makes itself at home when suited. Early-flowering herbaceous plants of some size like these, other than spring bulbs, are always welcome and these come out with the late bluebells.

ARISAEMA. Here are lovely arums to associate in a shady border woodland glade with ferns and Trilliums. All have typically spathed flowers but some are oddly hooded.

candidissimum   *1 × 1½ft (300 × 460mm.)   June–July*

Although a pure white form exists as the name suggests, the stiff spathe is usually flushed inside with pink and is green-striped outside. This exquisite flower emerges before the developing leaves, which are later themselves noteworthy; sometimes if one's plant is really happy spikes of red berries follow to give an autumn show.

triphyllum   *1 × 1ft (300 × 300mm.)   June–July*

This is the North American Jack in the Pulpit or Dragonroot. Here the narrow green-striped spathe is elegantly turned over the spadix, and in the form *zebrinum* has purple and white stripes very much in the fashion of Regency wall-paper. Other arisaemas from the Himalayas and Japan are sometimes on offer and should be snapped up at once. All are fascinating plants for sheltered shady nooks.

ARISARUM proboscideum   *6 × 6in. (150 × 150mm.)   May*

The 'proboscis' of the Latin epithet also provides our own name for this charming little thing — Mouse Plant. In any cool leafy spot it makes good ground-cover with small arrow-shaped leaves through which long tails appear as if a herd of mice were standing on their heads. Investigation will show them to be elongated ends of brown and white arum-spathes.

ARUM. Where leaves of Arisaemas are lobed or fingered those of true Arums are clearly arrow-shaped. Even our own native Lords and Ladies (*A. maculatum*) is in no way to be despised for woodland shade — the sight of the unfolding leaves shining in

January is one of the first signs that the year has turned, but better still is

italicum ADS   *1½ × 1ft (460 × 300mm.)   May*

which, although only rarely native with us, is the common arum of southern Europe. The flowers are typically araceous with somewhat floppy spathes, usually dull yellow but purplish to pink forms exist. They are followed by striking spikes of scarlet fruits (*not* to be taken internally) bright for some weeks from August. But it is the leaves, especially in the lovely marbled form 'Pictum', which are the prime attraction. They are well up in late November and continue to look fresh throughout winter. They make a lovely garden picture with Christmas roses, Corsican hellebore, a marbled ivy perhaps, and the earliest snowdrops.

ARUNCUS dioicus ADS   *6 × 4ft (2 × 1·2m.)   July*

A splendidly robust plant like a huge astilbe making a mound of elegant leaves above which come the high plumes of creamy white flowers. It is unusual as being dioecious (that is with separately sexed plants: the term monoecious, as in hazel or marrow, refers to separately sexed flowers on the same plant) with the male flower spikes being the more ornamental. It is happy in almost any position and especially good with rheums and petasites and other grand-leaved plants. 'Knieffii' is a delightful smaller form, only about half the size of the species.

ASARUM. The wild ginger of Canadian woods with highly aromatic heart-shaped leaves.

caudatum ADS   *9in. × 1ft (230 × 300mm.)   May*

Splendid tight growth of evergreen leaves which conceal the fleshy purplish urn-shaped flowers. *A. shuttleworthii* is similar; *canadense*, being deciduous, is less useful.

127

europaeum   *6 × 6in. (150 × 150mm.)   May*

Asarabacca, used medicinally, is a smaller plant but its leaves are so glossy as to pick up any light in the darkest spot.

ASPERULA odorata ADS   *6in × 2ft (150 × 600mm.)   May*

This is the lovely Sweet Woodruff and seldom can a name be more descriptive, referring here to its scent, habitat and the whorls of little leaves which support the white flowers. Although lovely it should not be introduced to the choicest shady borders because of its overweening ambition. Anywhere else a gem.

ASTILBE. There is now a wide range of these elegant moisture-lovers. Usually seen lining stream-sides or planted in broad swathes with irises and primulas it might be thought that they offer little to gardens unblessed with water. But this is just where shade is a virtue. So long as the organic content of the soil can be built up to hold moisture they are very happy in shady beds, either massed or when space is limited restricted to three or four plants of different flowering times, planted with an iris or a hellebore for foliage contrast.

Few plants have both such elegance of foliage and flower; the former is good from its bronzy unfurling to its dried winter state, while the flowers last for weeks and the dead spikes remain ornamental for months.

It is necessary to go to the nurserymen's lists to pick out types suitable for one's own needs. Astilbe hybrids (usually under the name of *A.* x *arendsii*) vary from 2 − 4ft. in height with a similar spread. The white and pale pink varieties usually have light green leaves while the darker pinks and red sport suitably dark foliage. Flowering time is from June to early August. Really dwarf forms, no more than a foot high, are now being raised, which are admirable for the front of shady borders and in scale with even the smallest garden.

ASTRANTIA. This is the old Masterwort of European wood-margins. A slightly surprising cow-parsley relative (Umbellifer) each of whose typical umbels of flowers is supported by a ring of bracts, providing a Victorian posy effect.

major ADS   *2 × 1½ft (600 × 460mm.)   July–September*

The flowers are white with greenish bracts in the usual form but pinkish and purplish variants are sometimes offered. The variegated-leaved Masterwort can be very striking but loses its brightness in deep shade.

maxima   *2 × 1ft (600 × 300mm.)   July–August*

A rather more distinguished plant though probably less easy to satisfy, liking a moister soil. The wide-spreading flower-bracts are clear pink.

BEGONIA

evansiana   *1 × 1ft (300 × 300mm.)   August–September*

It may seem something of a nonsense to be able to list a begonia which survives English winters but this really does succeed — even in a cold climate like that of Cambridge — in a protected spot in the shade of a wall shrub. The lovely, typically off-centre, leaves are pink underneath and the flowers repeat this colour.

BERGENIA ADS. One of the most valuable genera for ground cover in half-shade: splendid great leathery leaves from spreading woody rhizomes and profuse spikes of flowers in winter and spring. They are particularly good in association with building and paving, softening hard edges and enhancing steps and so on. Their ability to survive in the poorest conditions has done them no good; performance and beauty in good conditions are a revelation to anyone having seen them in the former state. Several named forms are now available and others will follow yet the species remain plants of great beauty.

129

ciliata   *1 × 1½ft (300 × 460mm.)   March*

Perhaps because it is rather tender and hence little seen this plant seems to have a definite quality the more robust types lack. The leaves are hairy and the heads of flowers pale pink to near white. Good for a sheltered shady courtyard. In the western Himalayas it grows on rock ledges at 10,000ft (3·2km.)

cordifolia   *1½ × 2ft (460 × 600mm.)   March–April*

Fine rounded leaves with crinkled edges and tall heads of mauve-pink flowers. The form 'Purpurea' is darker in flower and this colour is reflected in the shining red flower stalks. The leaves often turn purple in winter but the shadier the spot the less this will occur. *B. crassifolia* is rather similar though distinct: it helps to have the two together.

purpurascens   *1 × 1ft (300 × 300mm.)   March–April*

Good in flower but particularly useful for leaf colour in winter. The leaves redden even in shade. 'Sunningdale' inherits this characteristic in a generally better plant.

x schmidtii   *1½ × 2ft (460 × 600mm.)*

This lovely old hybrid is fine anywhere but with good cultivation and a warm garden it is possible to pick flowers at Christmas in most years. Then the clear pink flowers are on short stems but gradually they unfold into graceful sprays above the clear green leaves. The named clones are of mixed parentage and origin. Amongst the best are 'Abendglut', the smallest of the group whose leaves keep close to the ground. The flowers, often double, are deep purplish red. 'Ballawley' by comparison is a monster, 2ft high and the same across, but more diffuse and hence lighter in effect than most bergenias and also without much blue in its flowers. A lovely plant. 'Silberlicht' is invaluable as a white bergenia but is cursed with some of the frost-tenderness of *B. ciliata*.

BRUNNERA

macrophylla   *1½ × 1½ft (460 × 460mm.)   April–May*

Here is a lovely perennial forget-me-not, flowering with its unfolding leaves. These develop further to provide a good green ground-layer in woodland or under shrubs long after most such plants have gone down for their summer rest. The variegated form is much less robust, good as the herbaceous layer of a stratified association in a sheltered courtyard.

BUGLOSSOIDES rubro-coeruleum (Lithospermum), ADS
1 × 3ft (300 × 900mm.)   June

A splendid colonizer under trees even in dry soil with long horizontal growths arching along and rooting the while. Heads of dark blue borage flowers.

CALTHA palustris.   *1 × 1½ft (300 × 460mm.)   April–May*

This is the well-known Kingcup of our marshy meadows. In a pondless garden a shady corner can be made moist enough to accommodate this with an iris or two and some primulas. The charming double form is tighter in habit and better for a restricted spot.

CAMPANULA. By contrast all bell flowers need well-drained soil. Several happily take shade and are good under shrubs and in light tree shade.

glomerata   *2 × 1½ft (600 × 450mm.)   June–July*

Garden forms of our native Clustered Bellflower such as 'Superba' are very useful in borders where a tendency to greed is not a vice. Such a tendency increases to a certainty in *C. rapunculoides* and *C. trachelium*, but their lovely spikes of blue are valuable under trees, in thin orchard grass and big shrub borders where, at ground level, only spring bulbs need to try to compete.

lactiflora   *4 – 5 × 2ft (1·2 – 1·5m. × 600mm.)   June–July*

This is one of the loveliest of plants, with great sprays of lilac flowers (or pink in 'Loddon Anna'). Amongst tall earlier-flowering shrubs or, again, in orchard grass, it is beautiful with lilies and lupins. It will also do well under trees if the canopy is high.

latifolia   *4 × 2ft (1·2m. × 600mm.)   July*

A British native of northern hedge banks and hence is happy to be given some shade further south. In spite of a dangerous nearness in name to the preceding, in habit it is very different, standing strongly upright.

persicifolia   *3 × 1ft (900 × 300mm.)   June–July*

This old cottage-garden plant is always useful, amongst shrubs, following bulbs, under roses — especially old-fashioned roses — with its thin-leaved spikes of large open bells. A garden will soon develop colour variants from white to dark blue from self-sown seedlings. All are beautiful and the best should be encouraged.

CARDAMINE

pratensis   *3 – 4 × ½ft (1 – 1·2m. × 150mm.)   May*

The damp watermeadows where this lovely little plant used to be so common are less frequently seen. In moist half-shade both the species and its double-flowered form are always a gentle pleasure.

CAREX pendula ADS   *4 × 3ft (1·2 × 1m.)   July onwards*

Our most distinguished sedge, a plant of damp woodland making fine clumps of wide grassy leaves and tall, gracefully arching spikes of flowers which last, alive or dead, for months. In cultivation it will take far drier conditions than it inhabits in the wild. A lovely plant for associating with heavier-leaved things.

CHAEROPHYLLUM

hirsutum 'Roseum' *2 × 1ft (600 × 300mm.) May*

This is the pink form of a common hedge-row cow-parsley. Called more grandiloquently 'Pink Queen Anne's Lace' it would probably get more takers and once better known get the use it deserves.

CHELIDONIUM

majus *1½ × 1½ft (460 × 460mm.) June–July*

Another native plant, this is the Greater Celandine (actually a poppy) whose orange sap is reputed to cure warts. The yellow flowers are nothing much but the glaucous ferny leaves are very attractive, and it is happy under shrubs or in open woodland. Root growth appears thin and thus it competes little, even when seeding about, with other things, and the excess seedlings are so easily removed that they cause no problems.

CHRYSANTHEMUM. The conventional autumn-flowering chrysanthemums are not plants for shade but the genus is a large one and offers several good plants for our needs.

corymbosum ADS *3½ × 1½ft (1·15m × 460mm.)*
July–August

This has been in our gardens for centuries but even now is not common. It is a simple plant and easy to grow and rather resembles a giant feverfew.

macropyllum ADS *4 × 2ft (1·2m. × 600mm.) July–August*

A rather similar but even bigger plant though with heads of flowers that are a less pure white. The leaves are agreeably aromatic.

parthenium ADS   *2 × 1ft (600 × 300mm.)   July–September*

This is the old herb Feverfew which has developed a rather doubtful reputation lately, not as a febrifuge as its name suggests, but as a migraine cure. While it has undoubtedly helped some sufferers it has left others with equally unpleasant mouth ulcers so it is best left as an ornamental garden plant until medical research clarifies the situation. The species is a pretty thing with ferny leaves and diffuse heads of white single daisies. A golden-leaved form comes true from seed and so do semi and fully double types. They need good drainage and seed themselves around.

CIMICIFUGA. A group of valuable, though still uncommon, plants which provide height without bulk. Late summer spikes of creamy white fuzzy flowers are like soft bottle-brushes. Moist half-shade is ideal.

racemosa   *5 × 2ft (1·5m. × 600mm.)   July–August*

The earliest to flower and most generally available. Other good species are *C. simplex* and *C. ramosa*, which if discovered should be bought at once.

CLINTONIA. A North American genus for a cool woodland spot or shady bed devoted to choice things. They need lime-free leafy soil. Belonging also to the Liliaceae, foliage is rather lily-of-the-valley like, but bigger, and the nodding flowers (pink in *C. andrewsiana* and green-yellow in the commoner *C. borealis*) are succeeded — if the not very easy plants succeed at all — by blue berries.

CODONOPSIS. A group of delicate Asiatic bell flowers, cream, pale or darker blue, and all with extraordinary rings of different colours, orange, near black, greenish, inside the bell. Two are twiners (*C. convolvulacea* and *C. vinciflora*) and others such as *C. clematidea* and *C. ovata* are free standing but not robust, so all are best amongst low shrubs where they can scramble or find support. They go down completely in winter to brittle roots (resembling unsuccessful bellbine) so need careful marking if they are not to be weeded out by mistake.

CONVALLARIA. No garden of whatever size can be complete without Lily of the Valley though the plant itself may well reject a lot of sites offered to it. Where happy it will romp about under shrubs and come up in gravel paths. As a natural woodlander a leafy well-drained soil seems ideal to start with though where it will move to is its own affair.

majalis   *9 × 9in (230 × 230mm.)   May*

The typical plant with its exquisite scent is varied by 'Fortin's Giant', bigger in all its parts and flowering a week or so later, thus invaluable for extending the season, and by 'Rosea' a dusky pink. *C. m. Variegata* with gold-banded leaves is lovely, for it flowers as well as the type, but the variegation is not always very permanent and even less so in shade.

CORYDALIS. A group of plants for thin woodland or under shrubs to associate with the smaller spring bulbs. All have lovely lacy leaves and spikes of flowers like miniscule antirrhinums.

bulbosa   *9 × 12in (230 × 300mm.)   March–April*

This and the even smaller *C. solida* have pale purple flowers and are good, because so different in form, mixed with the more conventional small early spring bulbs. Like them they are out of sight by the end of June.

COTULA ADS Two or three little New Zealand carpeters which will cover soil with ferny leaves and rooting as they go. Not for choice borders but useful where, for instance, annual meadow grass would otherwise come in and be its normal nuisance self.

CROCOSMIA. This is today's generic name for what we usually call Montbretias. There are not many South Africans which do not prefer full sun so these are valuable in providing, for half-shade at least, a shape and texture in foliage which is unusual in such a situation.

CURTONUS *4 × 1ft (1·2m. × 300mm.)   August*

An old name *Antholyza* provided the common name by which it is affectionately known: Aunt Eliza. Its sword-like leaves are ribbed and more upright than with the Montbretias but the tall sprays of flowers are just as fine. It is robust enough to continue to thrive in disused cottage gardens with Monkshood and other such traditional plants in half-shade.

CYPRIPEDIUM. Anyone with a bit of cool woodland or a shady bed of cherished gems will want to try the exquisite hardy Lady's Slipper Orchids. But to obtain them is not easy, even less to be reasonably sure that the stock is a good one and with care will survive.

There are several species, all lovely, the flowers made up of a pouch and surrounding petals contrasting in colour. The height and spread of a successful clump are a foot or so each way. *C. calceolus* is such a rare British native that the number of wild specimens in existence can be numbered on the fingers of one hand. (William Curtis in the late eighteenth century was shocked even then to see a man selling plants rooted up from the Yorkshire woods in Settle market-place). Fortunately it is commoner in continental Europe. Other species are native to North America and to the Far East. But again, for the most part, in spite of statutory protection, plants on offer are probably wild and a moral quandary exists whether one should buy them or not.

DACTYLORRHIZA. A small group of lovely orchids which used to be grouped under Orchis itself. If leafy soil is moist enough they will enjoy almost full sun but in most situations half-shade is accepted and they associate well with the primulas and so on that like similar conditions.

elata   *2½ × 1ft (760 × 300mm.)   June*

A fine tall spike of dark pink flowers which lasts for some time. A similar but rather smaller orchid from Madeira (the other is Algerian) is variable in colour from pale pink to deep purple.

DEINANTHE

coerulea   *1½ × 1½ft (460 × 460mm.)   July*

A true woodlander from China, needing shade and protection. It is a curious plant, with nodding, almost spherical flowers like those of *Kadsura*, blue-grey in colour, above the relatively large leaves.

DELPHINIUM must be mentioned as a lovely genus of herbaceous plants. All prefer sun and a shady garden must use the best Monkshoods for tall blue spikes. Borders which get a bit of sun at some part of the day, however, and are without over-hanging branches, can offer homes to those species available (though not the red Californians) or to the smaller modern strains such as Belladonna hybrids.

DENTARIA

pinnata   *1½ × 1ft (460 × 300mm.)   March*

A white crucifer like a bigger version of our *Cardamine pratensis* (q.v.) to which it is closely related. The name, or its translation to Toothwort, refers to the white tuberous roots. Good for a bit of early whiteness that is not supplied by bulbs.

DICENTRA. These charming poppy relatives enjoy cool shady borders. Above ferny foliage the flower stems arch and carry the flowers dangling below. Edward Lear's famous 'Nonsense Botany' plant, *Manypeeplia upsidedownia*, is a direct crib, unless, of course, it happened the other way round.

formosa   *1½ × 1½ft (460 × 460mm.)*   *May–June*

This is the easiest species and has lovely blue-green leaves and typically pink-mauve flower scapes. When happy it spreads widely but not invasively. Particularly good named clones are 'Adrian Bloom' and 'Pearl Drops'. *D. eximea* is more delicate in all its parts.

spectabilis   *2 × 1½ft (600 × 450mm.)*   *May–June*

One of the classic cottage garden plants that seems to be less happy anywhere else. It needs a cool spot but where the fat flowers get a gleam of sun it brightens their rose to crimson. It must have more common names than most other plants, from Bleeding Heart and Dutchman's Breeches to Lyre Flower and Lady in the Bath (the latter becomes clear if an upright flower is gently pulled open).

DIGITALIS purpurea. Our native foxglove is an invaluable woodland plant varying in colour from the typical rosy purple to white and with strains such as 'Excelsior Hybrids' bringing in pale yellow and near buff. All are beautifully marbled and spotted in the throat. While the hybrid strains are magnificent plants (up to 6ft (2m.) high) with flowers all round the stem it must be said that they lack the grace of the wildling with its one-sided spike. All are biennial. Thus the first year it is necessary to buy a few plants *and* sow seed to provide flower for year two. Subsequently they will seed themselves about and only need thinning out or moving to where they are most wanted.

There are several perennial species from southern Europe which in general need more sun. But the charming pale yellow

D. grandiflora likes half shade as does its odd cross with the common foxglove. This is

D. x **mertonensis**, which has large flowers on squat spikes of a sort of squashed strawberry colour. Although strictly perennial it needs frequent propagation: thin dry soil does not suit it.

DIPHYLLEIA

cymosa *2 × 1ft (600 × 300mm.)* *July*

Another unusual North American woodlander for the ideal cool leafy spot. The flowers are rather by the way, but a striking late-summer picture is made when the heads of vivid blue berries are held above the great bi-lobed leaves.

DODECATHEON. North Americans related to and enjoying similar conditions to candelabra primulas: humus and moisture with shade in inverse proportion to the other desiderata. Unlike primulas the petals are sharply reflexed cyclamen-wise to provide the apt name 'Shooting Stars'.

meadia *1½ × 1ft (460 × 300mm.)* *May–June*

There are several species, of which this isthe most robust and generally available. Pink and yellow flowers.

DORONICUM. In spite of its name, Leopard's Bane, it seems to have no reputation, like Wolf's Bane (q.v.), of being deadly poisonous. Anyway it is for looking at. All species have bright yellow daisies early in the year and give interest under shrubs, in shady borders or even in open woodland and orchard grassland. With their branching stems above heart-shaped leaves the show lasts for weeks.

'Miss Mason' *1½ × 2ft (460 × 600mm.)* *April–May*

An old garden plant of unknown origin, it is still one of the best.

pardalianches   *3 × 2ft (900 × 600mm.)   April–May*

A splendid spreader to put with spring bulbs in woodland, from whose earlier show it takes over: lovely with bluebells.

plantagineum 'Harpur Crewe'   *2½ × 1ft (760 × 300mm.)*
April–May

Another fine old plant, with bigger individual flowers, still of the same rich yellow.

DUCHESNEA indica. ADS A major disappointment. This plant covers ground looking just like a prolific alpine strawberry. The fruits look inviting but are disgusting. Much better plant Fragaria proper (q.v.).

EOMECON

chionanthum   *1½ × 1½ft (460 × 460mm.)*

Another charming poppy relative, this time from eastern China, for woodland or under shrubs. The smooth round leaves are topped by pure white nodding flowers, rather like a big wood anenome.

EPIMEDIUM. Considering the beauty of this group of plants in flower and foliage, and their ease of growth as well as their value as ground cover in shade, it is truly extraordinary that they are not commonly seen in 'ordinary gardens'. Botanically related to the barberries (a generally shrubby family), their flowers, on wiry spikes, more closely resemble small columbines and have a similar charm. All make tight ground cover and increase rather slowly by shallow-growing rhizomes.

Apart from *E. perralderanum*, which is a valuable evergreen, epimediums have a seasonal growth pattern which is itself a pleasure to observe. If last year's dead leaves are cut away in March (or before in an early season) the flower stems are seen to unfurl. Gradually the leaves follow, initially soft and delicate yet gradually attaining a wiry strength. Throughout the summer there is solid ground-cover towards a foot high. Then in late autumn the leaves take on further colours. Altogether an invaluable group for all shade needs: they divide easily.

To avoid repetition all can be taken as attaining a foot or so and flowering in April. The best include *E. grandiflorum*, crimson, and its variants 'Rose Queen' and 'White Queen'. *E. perralderanum* and *E.* x *versicolor* 'Sulphureum' are yellow. *E.* x *rubrum* is the smallest, with pink and white flowers. A particular favourite is *E. youngianum* 'Niveum' with relatively large white flowers above pale green foliage. The flower shape recalls those rather extraordinary caps worn by female members of high-church choirs.

EUPHORBIA. There can be few genera which exhibit so wide a range of forms, from little annual weeds of our gardens to Christmas-card poinsettias and great cactus-like trees of the African bush. One of the most obvious things that joins the spurges is the poisonous white latex which exudes from any cut surface. As might be expected all garden situations are needed to encompass a range and within this are several highly desirable shade plants.

amygdaloides   *1½ × 1ft (460 × 300mm.)   March–April*

It is suitable that the first to be listed is a British native. Not a spectacular plant, the woodspurge nonetheless has a real quiet charm: if it is already on one's ground one can be sure that good conditions exist for other woodlanders. There are purple-leaved and variegated forms rarely available. Desirable but difficult to get and nowhere near as robust as their parent.

griffithii   *3 × 2ft (900 × 600mm.)   June*

A Himalayan whose heads of orange-red come as close as we can get to a hardy poinsettia. Usually seen in herbaceous borders, it is also effective under shrubs. Mr Graham Thomas recommends it with yellow azaleas in half shade.

palustris ADS   *3½ × 3ft (1 × 1m.)   May*

A robust spurge with fine heads of bitter-yellow and good foliage which turns yellow in the autumn. As its name suggests as a marsh plant it likes moisture yet, surprisingly perhaps, it seems to succeed happily in dry soil in full shade. In such a position its impression of lushness is particularly valuable. The smaller green and yellow *polychroma* behaves similarly though too much shade causes etiolated growth and the typical dome of colour is lost.

robbiae ADS   *2 × 2ft (600 × 600mm.)   April–May*

One of the best plants for shade. In moist or dry soil it colonizes as much space as it is allowed, with its rosettes of dark green leaves on foot-high stems and clear green flower spikes above.

sikkimensis   *4 × 1½ft (1·2 × 460mm.)   May–June*

Tall stems of typical greenery-yallery spurge flowers are good, but more unusual is the early growth with red stems and white-veined leaves.

FILIPENDULA. These are the native and exotic meadow-sweets. Often confused with Astilbe (which has pointed plumes of flowers) these have flat plates of flowers, equally tiny. The leaves are truly very similar though on a larger scale, the whole building up very handsome plants.

palmata   *4 × 2ft (1·2m. × 600mm.)   July*

Although a couple of named forms are occasionally offered, the type is fine enough and a good clear pink. *F. purpurea* is similar but flowers a little earlier, the colour a rather fierce cherry-red which a shady woodland position helps to cool.

rubra   *6 × 4ft (2 × 1·2m.)   July*

This is an enormous plant and needs companions to scale if it is not to dominate too aggressively. But it is lovely in a moist position, by a woodland pool with rheums and peltiphyllums, perhaps, and big-leaved rhododendrons behind, to which it gives interest after their season is past.

FRAGARIA vesca is the little wild strawberry, happily running about under trees, its starlike flowers out from April to October followed of course by tiny but delicious fruit. The white fruited form is the one to get as the birds sit around waiting for it to ripen and hence give the grower a sporting chance.

GALAX

urceolata   *1½ × 1ft (460 × 300mm.)   June*

A fine evergreen carpeter from the Liquidambar and Lirodendron woodlands of eastern North America, where it covers large areas with its round evergreen leaves. Here we are pleased if one good clump gets going, but in acid leaf-litter it will spread slowly, putting up spires of small white flowers. Leaves of plants which get a bit of sun often turn bronze in autumn. The earlier name *G. aphylla* is still in common use.

GENTIANA. Most gentians — at least those commonly seen — are dwarf plants of high exposed uplands where shade is unknown. Yet one species is amongst the loveliest of all shade-lovers.

asclepiadea   *2 − 3 × 2ft (600 − 900 × 600mm.)   August–September*

The Willow Gentian has pairs of narrow leaves throughout the length of the gently arching stems and the top dozen pairs carry flowers in their axils. These are typically mid-blue but darker and paler, as well as white, forms exist. As it is not difficult to grow from seed this should be sown (as soon as it is ripe and the pots left outside all winter) from one's first bought plants to build up a stock. Worthwhile variants may well appear. While

143

the Willow Gentian will grow in the dry shade even of Holm Oaks it develops its full size and grace in moister leafy soil and is worth every care. Lime is no problem.

GERANIUM with Bergenia and Helleborus one of the most valuable herbaceous genera for shady places. Those which accept shade, and that is most of them, are also good carpeters, keeping their leaves for all or much of the year. The floral display is by no means inconsiderable so long as no comparison is made with florists' 'geraniums' (actually Pelargonium). And then it is a moot point as to which is the more desirable.

endressii *1½ × 2ft (460 × 600mm.)   June–October*

From the Pyrenees, this is one of the finest Geraniums for half-shade with its bright pink flowers held well above the elegant leaves. If planted under trees in informal areas it will move out into empty places in the sun but probably prefers, and certainly looks better, in the cool. Several forms have been selected for futher flower colour. 'A. T. Johnson' is silvery pink while 'Wargrave Pink' is a stronger tint approaching salmon. Both are also bigger in growth than the type, providing vigorous ground cover. 'Claridge Druce' is a hybrid with *G. endressii* in it; here the luxuriant foliage is greyish green, admirably setting off the blue-pink flowers.

'Johnson's Blue' *1 × 2ft (300 × 600mm.)   June–July*

Another splendid hybrid. This time the parents are **himalayense** (itself worth growing) and our own big Meadow Cranesbill. Good ground cover and dark-veined lavender-blue flowers.

macrorrhizum ADS   *1 × 2ft (300 × 600mm.)   May–June*

A low ground-coverer with near-evergreen leaves although they also take on surprising autumn colour. The white form 'Album' and 'Ingwersen's Variety' are to be preferred to the type with its rather dull magenta flowers.

144

maculatum *2 × 1½ft (600 × 460mm.)   May–June*

A North American with good dissected leaves and rose pink flowers, earlier than most. It needs cool woodland soil.

x magnificum *2 × 2ft (600 × 600mm.)   June–July*

This is often listed as *G. ibericum platypetalum*. It has especially handsome leaves and dark lavender-blue flowers in quantity.

nodosum ADS *1½ × 1½ft (460 × 460mm.)   June–September*

Bushy little plants of glossy green leaves with lilac-blue flowers. Here it is possible to add that it thrives in dry shade, not merely accepting it with some reluctance as is often the case.

phaeum ADS *2 × 1½ft (600 × 450mm.)   May–June*

Opening its first flowers in late April in warm spots this is perhaps the earliest cranesbill to bloom. The flowers are held well above the foliage and hold their petals reflexed behind a forward-pointing boss of stamens. There are white, mauve and nearly black forms. All are beautiful.

pratense *2 × 2ft (600 × 600mm.)   July–September*

The Meadow Cranesbill is one of our most beautiful wild plants, showing off its twopence-sized blue flowers particularly well against the lush greenness of our northern hedge-banks. Its preference for the cooler north makes it admirable for open woodland or in orchard grass. In borders the lovely double forms spread with less freedom and are thus to be preferred, as are two fine plants from northern India (this species has an enormous geographical distribution) sold as 'Kashmir Purple' and 'Kashmir White'.

psilostemon ADS *3 × 3ft (1 × 1m.)   July–August*

In spite of Miss Jekyll's damning phrase 'malignant magenta' (she didn't go in for barring holds) this is one plant where the colour is better described as 'magnificent magenta' emphasized as it is by the black eye of every flower. All this above a great heap of fine leaves. In dryish shade it gets less big and looks lovely with yellow and orange Welsh poppies seeding about.

renardii   *1 × 1ft (300 × 300mm.)   June–July*

A good low colonizer with rounded grey-green leaves and dark-veined flowers of the palest possible purple.

sanguineum   *1 × 1ft (300 × 300mm.)   June–July*

The Bloody Cranesbill, an uncommon native still to be found in the grykes of the limestone pavements in Lancashire. The lovely pale pink 'Lancastriense', although in cultivation since the early eighteenth century, still grows wild there. A good white form is taller but flops rather.

wallichianum ADS   *1 × 2ft (300 × 600mm.)   July–October*

In the form 'Buxton's Variety' this is one of the top plants for half or full shade. Clear blue open flowers with white eyes are carried for months above good ground-covering foliage.

GEUM.   The bigger-flowered chiloense hybrids such as 'Lady Stratheden' and 'Mrs Bradshaw' (orange-yellow and brick-red respectively) are some of the best plants for conventional herbaceous border requirements in shade, flowering from May to October. *G.* x *borisii*, another old hybrid, is a lovely soft orange.

rivale   *1 × 1ft (300 × 300mm.)   April–June*

Our native Water Avens (known in America as Indian Chocolate) with pleasant nodding flowers of a purplish, buffish pink is good in moist shade in an unspectacular way. More noticeable is the hybrid with the Wood Avens, *Geum* x *intermedium*.

GLAUCIDIUM palmatum   *2 × 2ft (600 × 600mm.)   May*

Usually put in the Ranunculaceae, it is now sometimes accorded a family of its own, no doubt because of its four, not five, petals. These are pale lavender, the whole effect being rather meconopsis-like. Another plant for the shaded corner of gems in moist leafy soil — if ever it is available.

GLYCERIA maxima 'Variegata'   *2 – 4 × 1 – 2ft (600mm – 1.2m. × 300 – 600mm.)*

The wide divergence in estimates of size reveals that this normally vigorous waterside grass becomes positively restrained when grown, as it can be, in dry spots. This variegated garden form has cream-striped leaves which are at first bright pink as the shoots push up in the spring.

GUNNERA manicata   *6 × 8ft (2 × 2·5m.)   July*

A plant of the most enormous scale like a vast prickly rhubarb (to which it has no relationship at all). Normally seen close to water, any moist position will suit and half-shade is not objected to. It is naturalized in shady hedge banks in some of our warmer areas. The flower spikes are like huge cones inconspicuous in all but size. In cold areas the crowns should have a protective mulch, first of the dead leaves themselves and then of bracken or straw.

HELLEBORUS.

As a marvellous group of plants for shady borders and woodland in almost any soil except the driest and most acid, hellebores cannot be over-praised. Their value is continuous. There are no grander flowers for the open garden in winter, with a range of forms and colours which careful breeding and selection is still increasing. Unlike so many other plants this has in no way upset the natural poise and charm of the genus. Several of the species, notably the Corsican and *H. orientalis* seed themselves about in shade with gay abandon: the first comes perfectly true while the second will offer a wide range of colour forms, all worthwhile.

atrorubens *1 × 1½ft (300 × 460mm.) December–March*

A lovely deciduous Lenten Rose. Anticipating that festival by many weeks, it can often be picked for the feast of Christmas and lasts cut, incidentally, much more certainly than the rest of its group. Each flower stem carries up to 5 or 6 typically saucer-shaped flowers of dusky purple. By the time all are over the new leaves have risen up and provided a second picture.

corsicus *2 × 3ft (600 × 900mm.) December–April*

A plant which might be thought to decline into a garden cliché for being so universally admired. But here familiarity only breeds content — especially when it becomes at home enough to sow itself. It has an oddly biennial sub-shrubby habit. Spring growth produces strong woody shoots of striking saw-edged leaves. By autumn a fat central bud has developed at the top which bursts into a profuse head of flowers, depending upon strain, season and site, from November to April. They are clear pale green bowls with a boss of stamens enclosed by a ring of nectaries typical of the genus. The display lasts for months. As the seeds' capsules swell their weight causes the shoots to lean outwards leaving the centre open for the next season's growth. It is thus always in beauty.

Botanists now aver that the Corsican Hellebore is a geographical subspecies of the Majorcan *H. lividus.* This is less hardy but hybrids between the two are safe and inherit a pinkish flush to the flowers and, more important, a delicious marbling to the leaves.

foetidus *1½ × 1½ft (460 × 460mm.) January–March*

Another evergreen with fingered leaves on a woody stem topped with open heads of purple-edged green bells. The name need put off no one, the smell is not at all obtrusive and the plant (an uncommon native) is striking at all times. Selected forms such as 'Cabbage Stalk' are more vigorous and look splendid with bergenias and hostas.

niger   *1 × 1ft (300 × 300mm.)   December–April*

The exquisite Christmas Rose is a plant which everybody wants to grow — who can resist the great pure white bowls with their golden stamens appearing in the depths of winter? — but few are really good at keeping. It likes shade and moist leafy soil (and protection from slugs, which are as fond of it as we are). Important, too, is the form obtained: 'Potters Wheel' is the best of the named kinds. Most, it must be said, are less likely to provide flowers for the Christmas table than *H. atrorubens*.

Lovely but sterile crosses have been made between the Christmas Rose and the Corsican and may be found in one or two specialist catalogues under the name *H. x nigericors*.

orientalis   *1½ × 1½ft (460 × 460mm.)   February–April*

A number of possibly true species (*abschasicus*, *guttatus*, *kochii*) can be lumped together here as Lenten Roses, providing a group of completely beautiful hardy plants. The seasonal growth pattern is like that of the Corsican but the fine palmate leaves and flower stems arise separately from the root stock: by flowering time last year's leaves are nearly flat upon the ground. New growth makes a great dome of green.

Flower colour varies from palest primrose-green through white, pink to darkest sloe-purple. All are variously speckled inside and all are lovely.

viridis   *1 × 1ft (300 × 300mm.)   February–March*

This is the second native hellebore and its habitat of moist woodland on rather heavy alkaline soil indicates its likes. It is deciduous, on a much smaller scale than the rest, but the bare flower stems of avocado-green flowers are no less lovely.

HEMEROCALLIS.   For shade the Day Lilies are almost as important for their foliage as for their flowers, and its effect is certainly longer lasting. The elegant grassy clumps start to grow very early in the year and are brightly pale. The bigger species can be rather invasive but under trees and big shrubs or in old orchard grass this is no sin. For smaller gardens and choice sites there are also suitable types. Individual flowers are, of course, literally ephemeral, but their succession provides colour for a considerable time; a chosen selection could give flower from May to July.

dumortieri   *2 × 1½ft (600 × 460mm.)*   *May*

This and the smaller *H. minor* are elegant perennials for early effect, taking over from the spring bulbs and forming good compact clumps. Good with *Symphytum grandiflorum* clustering around.

flava   *2 × 1½ft (600 × 460mm.)*   *May–June*

This lovely old garden plant has been with us since Elizabethan times and still earns its keep in big gardens. Yellow fragrant flowers held well above the foliage.

fulva   *3½ × 2ft (900 × 600mm.)*   *July*

Another old plant which John Gerard (of 'Herbal' fame) grew in his garden at Holborn. They are a sort of orange-suède colour of lovely shape and poise. The spreading clumps of wide grassy leaves will grow in odd half-shady corners and always catch the eye. There is a double form and one with pink flowers which is a parent of so many modern cultivars.

These are now available in a wide range of colour, yellows, oranges, pinks and dark reds, often with a different reverse to the petals. One should go to a nursery which offers them or a garden possessing a range to pick out one's favourites. These modern hybrids are generally less vigorous than the types, which have stood the test of centuries.

7 The exquisite flowers of *Dicentra spectabilis* swing in the slightest
   breeze.

8 A north-east facing corner in an old walled garden. Dramatic big
   leaved plants, Ligularia, Gunnera and Hosta, get a gleam of sun at
   noon in high summer.

9 In the shade of an Almond tree, *Euphorbia robbiae, Hemerocallis* and *Symphytum grandiflorum* combine.

10 Most lilies benefit from shade at the root and dappled sun at the flower.

11 *Primula florindae,* the easiest and most robust of Himalayan primroses.

12 *Aruncus dioicus* and giant hogweed in a chalky dell provide a cool effect on the hottest day.

13 Green-leaved forms of *Aucuba japonica* show off the fruit to best advantage.

HERACLEUM mantegazzianum *10 × 5ft (3 × 1·5m.) July*

A vast cow parsley from the Caucasus which seeds itself in open woodland with decent moist soil. Not a plant for small gardens — as Mr Thomas has so rightly remarked it is ideal for decorating the Royal Albert Hall — nor where it might compete with smaller things. It should not be meddled with on hot days when its sap can bring up on bare skin suitably Herculean blisters.

HEUCHERA. Cottage garden plants resembling London Pride with good foliage and spires of small flowers for the front of shady borders. *H. americana* is grown especially for its satiny hummocks of ivy-shaped leaves. Heuchera has also been crossed with Tiarella to give the attractive little bi-generic hybrid, x *Heucherella*.

sanguinea *1 × 1ft (300 × 300mm.) June–July*

Known as Coral Bells, this pretty plant has been given the 'Bressingham Treatment' and produced some excellent garden plants. It can be taken as axiomatic that clonal names prefixed by 'Bloom' or 'Bressingham' are safe bets.

HOSTA. A shady garden without hostas is inconceivable. Their lustrous broad leaves provide marvellous garden contrast with other shade-lovers — ferns or hemerocallis — and are also invaluable cut for the house. Colours vary through shades of green and near-blue, while others offer astonishing variegated forms. Flower spikes, which may be up to nearly 3 feet/1m. high, carry lily-like trumpets in shades of purple and pale lavender paling to white; it should be noted, however, that the best flowering hosta, *H. plantaginea*, is not a plant for shade.

All the others, however, flourish in shady borders and even under trees if not too dry. Here, however, smooth-leaved types such as *H. lancifolia, crispula* and *ventricosa* are best. Profusion of flower is likely to be in inverse proportion to depth of shade, but leaves may well be bigger and finer. Those with puckered leaves (the ones to avoid under trees) are known aptly in America as Seersucker Plantain Lilies.

151

Hostas have been a part of the Japanese garden scene for centuries and it was from Japanese gardens that the original early nineteenth-century introductions came which explains the unusual situation of variegated forms having full specific status. As all hostas are good it is probably sufficient here to group the few readily available according to size.

Small Hostas, *1½ × 1½ ft (460 × 460mm.)*

albomarginata.   Good glossy oval leaves with pronounced white edge. Spikes of purple flowers. There is a green-leaved white-flowered type.

lancifolia.   A dark-flowered green-leaved plant which puts up a good late display even under trees in dry soil.

undulata.   Another variegated plant but here the creamy, non-photosynthetic area is the leaf centre. Leaves are noticeably twisted.

Mid Size, *2 × 2ft (600 × 600mm.)*

Fine white-edged plants include *H. crispula* and *H. decorata*. *Fortunei* has a range of forms both green and variegated but the finest (some would say of all hostas) is *H. f. albopicta*: here the rolled leaves open to clear yellow which gradually fades while a green edge darkens. As the season advances the leaves become soft green all over. Above this the flowers are palest purple.

Big Hostas, *2½ – 3 × 2ft (760mm. – 1m. × 600mm.)*

H. sieboldiana in foliage is the grandest of all, with huge heart-shaped leaves a foot across and of a marvellous glaucous blue. 'Frances Williams' is an American selection with a gold edge. Gardens which cannot give room to such a vast plant should try to obtain the lovely *H. tokudama* — half the size and just as blue — but it is rare and probably expensive.

A great virtue of hostas is their ease of cultivation and increase (Mr Thomas recommends chopping bits out of established clumps in spring 'as one would cut a slice out of a round cake'. The slice is transplanted and its hole filled in with good compost and no harm done). Seeds of those which are fertile can be used to produce quantities of plants for mass plantings: three years are needed, however, before their ground cover is effective.

HOUTTOYNIA cordata *1 × 1ft (300 × 300mm.)*
July– August

The dark heart-shaped leaves topped by pure white flowers are effective in moist shady spots. A double form is even better but both can be rather invasive.

HYLOMECON japonicum *1 × 1ft (300 × 300mm.) April*

A Japanese woodlander for a shady spot which is rather like a taller yellow wood anemone. It slowly makes a good clump and flowers for some time.

IRIS. The vertical emphasis which monocotyledons supply to the garden scene and which is so important for contrast is provided admirably by many irises. While the majority, however, are sun-lovers a few can be included here.

confusa *3 × 3ft (1 × 1m.) May*

Without doubt this is one of the most striking irises. It enjoys sun but more important is a protected spot. Thus it is a good courtyard plant for warmer parts of the country in half shade where the evergreen fans of leaves held upon bamboo-like stems make the maximum effect. Sprays of flat blue, white and yellow flowers come from each leaf-fan and as they go over the foliage growth is renewed from the base rather as *Helleborus corsicus* behaves. At no time, therefore, is the clump unattractive.

foetidissima ADS   *1½ × 1½ft (460 × 460mm.)   June*

A native plant with good evergreen foliage, rather insignificant flowers of a dusky buff-purple but superb pods opening to show off brilliant orange seeds. The show lasts for months from October, if flower arrangers can be kept at bay.

'Citrina' is bigger in all its parts and with more noticeable, paler, flowers. It is worth seeking out, as is 'Variegata', with fine white-banded leaves. This unfortunately fails to set seed. All are happy in deep shade in moist or dry soil and are very useful plants.

germanica ADS   *2½ × 1ft (760 × 900mm.)   May–June*

The old purple flag iris is the easiest of plants and will take dry half-shade under trees here just as one sees it in its southern European home. *I. florentina*, Orris-root, with white flowers, is equally accommodating. The hybrid flags are not suitable.

pseudacorus   *4 × 1ft (1·2m. × 300mm.)   May/June*

The wild yellow riverside flag is good if space is available in moist half shade but is too big and coarse for most garden scenes. Its golden variegated form, however, is perfectly acceptable in a moist north-facing border.

KIRENGESHOMA palmata   *3½ × 2ft (1m. × 600mm.)*
September–October

Here is one of the plants which, admired in another garden, makes one insist on a shady border. Elegant black stems carry rather vine-like leaves and diffuse sprays of bantam-egg-sized and -shaped flowers of clear buttermilk yellow. Coming up through hostas the effect is superb, particularly if the flowers can catch a gleam of late evening sun.

LAMIASTRUM galeobdolon. ADS *1ft (300mm.) × infinity April*

The variegated yellow Archangel is one of the most marvellous plants for ground cover under trees: marbled leaves and spikes of yellow flowers. But it is not for small gardens without constant cutting back or for putting with small shrubs, over which it will climb to give the effect of a muster of moles behaving badly under an eiderdown.

LAMIUM. The dead nettles are admirable ground cover in shade with hellebores, for example, and summer snowflake; they are too strong for small spring bulbs.

maculatum *3 – 4 × 2ft (1–1·2m. × 600mm.) May*

The wild type with marbled leaves and mauve flowers seems rather more vigorous than its pink- and white-flowered forms and much more than the golden one. Particularly striking is the fully silver type called 'Beacon Silver'. 'Chequers' is also good.

LIGULARIA. A genus which used to be amalgamated with Senecio. They are all great strong plants with fine heads of yellow or orange daisies in summer; much moisture is required and as its availability declines so progressively is the need for shade.

dentata *4 × 2ft (1·2m. × 600mm.) July–August*

In the shade of shrubs near water this is one of the most striking of summer flowers with its great flat heads of orange daisies: it will survive neglect and still appear with all the typically invasive waterside plants. For north-facing borders in more sophisticated surroundings the rather smaller purple-leaved cultivars 'Othello' and his inamorata, 'Desdemona', are more suitable.

'Gregynog Gold' is a remarkable hybrid between *L. dentata* and *L. veitchiana*, (itself well worth growing for its tall narrow spikes of flower). The hybrid is intermediate in shape of inflorescence. These are like orange pyramids above the strong round leaves.

przewalskii *6 × 3ft (2 × 1m.) July–August*

'The Rocket' is the best form of this elegant daisy. Tall black stems with narrow fingered leaves and thin spikes of yellow flowers.

LIRIOPE ADS.   A group of grassy-leaved perennials from the Far East with tight spikes of bead-like, usually blue, flowers in September and October. They flower poorly in deep shade but nonetheless manage to make reasonable ground cover. *L. muscari* is the best, the smaller *L. graminifolia* most accepting of poor conditions.

LOBELIA.   The tall perennial lobelias (utterly different from the blue part of conventional patriotic bedding schemes) are something of a snare. *L. cardinalis* is wild in Canada and hence puts up with much colder winters than ours, yet so erratic is the British climate that it is apt not to survive. But the summer scarlet spikes of this and the blue of *L. syphilitica* are well worth cherishing in a not too dark north-facing border. A range of hybrids is now available which may be less transitory: the royal-purple *L.* x *vedrariensis* is particularly good.

LUPINUS polyphyllus. Mr Russell's lovely selections (Russell Lupins have been a by-word for decades) are plants for sunny borders but the old blue species succeeds in thin orchard grass on well-drained soils and seeds itself around. Cut down after flowering in May and June a second crop will appear.

LYSICHITUM.   The bog arums. Great shield-like spathes in earliest spring emerge from bare ground and are succeeded by huge leaves, up to 3 feet/1m. long, which make a vast clump.

L. americana is bright yellow and the smaller (a mere 3 feet across the clump) *L. camtschatense* pure white. Along a woodland streamside nothing can be finer: when happy they seed themselves downstream.

LYSIMACHIA nummularia is the Creeping Jenny of our moist woods. It makes good ground-level cover with the bonus of shining yellow flowers. a gold-leaved form is very striking for deep moist shade.

clethroides   *2½ × 1½ft (760 × 460mm.)   August–September*

For late flower in a north border this is a favourite perennial. The spikes of white flowers are shaped like croziers carried by a bevy of bishops on church parade.

ephemerum   *2½ × 1ft (760 × 300mm.)   July–August*

Spikes of white flowers above grey foliage. Like anaphalis (q.v.) this is one of the few grey plants for shade.

punctata   *4 × 2ft (1·2m. × 600mm.)   July–August*

Strong yellow heads (each flower like that of Creeping Jenny) above an invasive pinkish rootstock. Another good plant for moist semi-shade in wild places.

LYTHRUM salicaria   *4 × 2ft (1·2m. × 600mm.)*
July–August

Purple Loosestrife is one of our most decorative waterside plants, with great spikes of brilliant pink. The colour is softened in half shade: 'Robert' has less of magenta about it. Planted by water the reflective effect is superb and is repeated in October when the foliage turns bright orange.

MACLEAYA.   It is scarcely believable that the name Plume Poppy really does state the botanical relationship of these tall plants with their feathery spikes of petal-less flowers. But the orange sap immediately recalls that of chelidonium (q.v.). The lovely milk white and grey-green leaves are also reminiscent. While not taking heavy shade they are fine amongst tall shrubs in light soil and will take their tops into the sun.

cordata   *6–7 × 2ft (2–2·2m. × 600mm.)   July–August*

Even in smaller gardens the height is not overpowering because of the light effect; nor does the plant run about aggressively as does the commoner

microcarpa   *7+ × 3ft (2·2+ × 1m.)   July–August*

Here the plumes are an unusual tone. 'Coral Plume' is even better. Still often listed as Bocconia.

MAIANTHEMUM bifolium   *½ × 1ft (150 × 300mm.)   May*

Like a smaller Lily of the Valley with upright leaves this is a worthwhile woodlander for cool spots under shrubs with trilliums and erythroniums. Often difficult to establish but when really suited it fairly roars away.

MECONOPSIS.   Anyone who sees for the first time the fabled Himalayan Blue Poppies really succeeding will rush back home to see if he can contrive a suitable site. This is the typical place that so much of this book is concerned with: shade, moisture, protection from wind and a leafy lime-free soil. The best-known species is

betonicifolia (baileyi)   *3–4 × 1½ft (1–1·2m. × 460mm.)*
June

When not really happy this beauty behaves monocarpically and dies after flowering. In the cooler north and west it is a perfectly good perennial with its yellow-centred clear blue flowers. Seed germinates with abandon but it is less simple to grow the plants on. Worth every effort and every care. The Branklyn forms are best.

cambrica   *1½ × 1ft (460 × 300mm.)   May–August*

The Welsh Poppy is a favourite easy seeder in shade or sun. Above a clump of elegant divided leaves the flowers are either soft orange or clear yellow. Both exist in double forms. It is lovely appearing in the cracks of paving, softening hard edges and blending with any colour but the hardest pinks.

grandis   *4–5 × 2ft (1.2–1.5m. × 600mm.)   June*

Even if it never flowered the handsome clumps of hairy leaves would be worth growing. As it does, with tall stems of blue, purple or white bowls, veined like Tiffany lamps, it is one of the joys of any garden that can offer the right conditions. The plant has a wide distribution in the upper Himalayan valleys of Sikkim, Nepal and Tibet and further collections, now that the areas are open again to botanists, may well offer more forms.

Hybrids between this and *M. betonicifolia* are usually grouped under *M.* x *sheldonii* and are splendid plants. It is recommended that the clumps be divided after flowering and carefully looked after until re-established.

MELISSA officinalis   *2 × 2ft (600 × 600mm.)   July*

The golden variegated form of Lemon Balm is invaluable for brightening a shady border and providing leaves to crush in the hand as one passes. In seeding it reverts to green and can become a nuisance.

MELITTIS melissophyllum ADS   *1½ × 1½ft (460 × 460mm.)   May–June*

Big pink and white dead-nettle flowers in the leaf axils make this rare native worthwhile under shrubs.

MENTHA. ADS   Mints, with Angelica, are of the few culinary herbs which accept shade. The ornamental-leaved types can be used culinarily so they are the ones to grow; they are also less susceptible to the unsightly mint rust disease. While revelling in moisture mints grow quite well in drier conditions but become less tall.

x gentilis *1½ × 1½ft (460 × 460mm.)   June–July*

This is Ginger Mint, the name referring not to its scent but leaf colour.

piperita var. citrata *2 × 1½ft (600 × 460mm.)   June–July*

The dark purple leaves and delicious scent of Eau de Cologne mint make it as distinctive in the hand as in the border.

x rotundifolia 'Variegata' *2 × 2ft (600 × 600mm.)   June–July*

Here by comparison the softly downy leaves are pale green and white with palest lavender flower spikes.

MERTENSIA virginica *1½ × 1ft (460 × 300mm.)   April*

This is the Virginian Cowslip — the sort of name expatriates take from favourite plants of their homeland — even when resemblance is more than a little tenuous, as here. Mertensia is that unusual creature, a smooth-leaved borage, with elegant drooping sprays of blue flowers. The white form has charm, but the blue is better.

MITELLA. Little white-flowered colonizers from North America which revel in cool woodland soil. *M. breweri* is most likely to be available.

MYOSOTIS.   Though not good perennials, any forget-me-not is worth encouraging to seed itself about with Welsh Poppies and suchlike.

MYRRHIS odorata *2½ × 2ft (760 × 600mm.)   May–July*

This elegant, aromatic cow-parsley shares northern hedge banks with *Geranium pratense* and spires of *Campanula latifolia*, and such an association could be repeated in a shady spot with advantage. Sweet Cicely has finely cut leaves and good heads of creamy flowers. There is then a choice: either the plant may be left to produce its surprisingly large black fruits or, as Miss Jekyll recommended, cut the whole thing to the ground, when a second crop of fresh green leaves will appear to enliven the late summer scene.

OMPHALODES. Two Venus' Navelworts (the name refers to the distinctive shape of the seeds) are admirable for the front of shady borders, the north side of rock gardens and similar spots. Both have broad leaves and clear blue forget-me-not flowers in spring. *O. verna* precedes *O. cappadocica*.

OURISIA. A couple of species from this attractive New Zealand genus used to flourish in the sandstone rock garden at Cambridge Botanic Garden — not a climate to encourage moisture-lovers. So, if available, the white *O. macrophylla* and scarlet *O. coccinea* might do well in other peaty shady spots and make good carpets of dark leaves. Good and permanent in south-west Scotland.

PAEONIA. The gorgeous genus of peonies offers little to the woodland garden proper but much to half-shady shrub borders where their early leaf growth and flowers enliven ground around deciduous shrubs. Some slight frost protection is also afforded thereby. Peonies in dry soil particularly appreciate some shade, which helps to retain the otherwise rather fleeting flowers. But flower is not all: developing leaves and swelling buds can be ravishing and scarlet seed-pods and blue seeds dramatic with the late-summer colouring foliage. These remarks apply particularly to the species and old hybrids. The modern hybrids enjoy more specialist treatment and positioning: for an account of these it is best to resort (as in so many things) to Mr Thomas's *Perennial Garden Plants*.

The following list includes most of the wild species which have a distribution from western Europe to eastern Asia. Few, it must be admitted, are generally available but seed sometimes is: a three-year-old plant has begun to develop a good flowering clump and it will increase in size and beauty from year to year.

cambessedesii   *1 × 1½ft (300 × 460mm.)   March–April*

This rare Balearic endemic has a reputation for frost-tenderness, as might well be expected. But in a sheltered place under shrubs, foliage begins to unfold even in January without appearing to come to harm. The leaves are an extraordinarily beautiful gunmetal grey above and beetroot beneath. The flowers are silvery rose — just the tint the most colour conscious person would choose on a good day. *P. russi* is rather similar but lacks some of the Majorcan's essential perfection.

daurica   *2½ × 2½ft (760 × 760mm.)   May*

This is lighter in effect with elegantly borne yellow-centred pinkish-white flowers above good green-fingered leaves with wavy edges.

lactiflora   *3 × 2ft (900 × 600mm.)   Late May*

A parent of most of the big Chinese hybrid peonies, yet it is as good as any. Foliage emerges and maintains a strong red tint against which the great white bowls of flowers are admirably set. Sometimes listed as *P. albiflora* and *P. whitleyi major*. *P. obovata alba* is another good white, smaller in stature with lovely dusky pink young growth.

mascula   *2 × 2ft (600 × 600mm.)   May*

is a variable southern European: in good forms the leaves are soft and waved, with a grey cast to set off the strong pink flowers.

mlokosewitschii   *2½ × 2½ft (760 × 760mm.)   Late April*

Such a splendid tongue-twister makes everyone remember this plant. And so we should. As the pale primrose flowers open to show the golden stamens we experience one of the exquisite moments of the garden year. Foliage is rounded, with pink stems, and has an overall air of softness.

officinalis *2 × 2ft (600 × 600mm.)   May*

The old herbalists' peony is less fleeting in flower than some of the foregoing and hence can take more sun. But it is still good under shrubs or in cottage garden orchard conditions or mixed up with the gooseberries and currants. The great double red is in the memory of everyone who has enjoyed a country garden childhood. There are pink and white forms, double and single.

tenuifolia *1½ × 1½ft (460 × 460mm.)   Early June*

One of the latest to flower. Dark red flowers glisten above fern-like foliage.

veitchii *1½ × 1½ft (460 × 460mm.)   Late May*

Slow to leaf, which could be an advantage in chilly areas, but develops quickly to show off its hanging flowers. These are a clear, unaggressive magenta.

wittmanniana *2½ × 2½ft (760 × 760mm.)   Early May*

The biggest in effect, with huge pale rounded leaves and cool yellow-cream flowers. Inside, the boss of stamens is green, lit up by the pink eyes of the stigmas. These lovely flowers are only at their best for a week but the build-up to flowering, the mature foliage and the seed-pods combine to give interest for months.

PELTIPHYLLUM peltatum *3 × 2ft (900 × 600mm.)   May*

Heads of bergenia-like pink flowers emerge from bare ground and only after they have finished do the leaves develop. They are worth waiting for: circular platters atop thick red stalks, hence the name Umbrella Plant. It needs a moist soil or water-side position, and it is in perfect scale with other big bog plants such as Lysichitum and Butterbur.

PENTAGLOTTIS semper virens ADS   *1½ × 2ft (460 × 600mm.)   May–June*

The Evergreen Alkanet is a typically bristly borage with bright blue flowers specking the spreading foliage. Common and rather aggressive but worth having in a neglected spot: good with Symphytum orientale.

PETASITES Dangerous plants to introduce into gardens because of their speed of increase but in moist soil under trees they are valuable and can look superb.

hybridus is the native Butterbur, with low cones of purple flowers (rayless daisies) in spring, followed by huge 2–3-foot (600–900mm.) wide leaves.

japonicus *3 × 5ft (1 × 1.5m.)   April*

is more ornamental in spring when the flower heads emerge from the bare soil. Each is perfect for a dinner-table decoration (talking from experience) when the host is in a hurry, resembling a carefully arranged posy of white surrounded by green leaves (in fact bracts). The monstrous ground-covering leaves follow.

PHLOX.   The big garden phloxes, forms of *P. paniculata*, in their splendid range of colour are not for overhead shade, though open north-facing borders suit them admirably, especially in less moisture-retentive soils. More suited to our needs are the elegant *P. maculata* types with longer, narrower heads of flowers. They do well in the north and Scotland.

PHYSALIS.   Chinese lanterns are surely less often seen than formerly. Perhaps the trend to smaller gardens has reduced their use. Certainly a big clump is needed to produce cutting material for winter decoration and it does look rather miserable in summer, with coarse leaves and little potato flowers. But when the leaves drop and the inflated capsules turn bright orange all is forgiven.

franchettii   *2 × 3ft (600 × 900mm.)*

This is the stronger species with one or two selected forms sometimes available. July flowers of no virtue.

PHYSOSTEGIA virginiana is the Obedient Plant whose salvia-like flowers can all be pushed to one side of the spike — where they unaccountably remain. The species is rather tall and coarse but a 2-ft (600mm.) white form and 'Vivid', smaller still, are lovely with Japanese Anemones in the front of a half-shady border in moist soil in autumn.

PODOPHYLLUM.   These unusual looking plants have a family to themselves, related to the *Berberidaceae*, which includes the epimediums (q.v.). Unfolding Podophyllum foliage has a similar texture and colouring, yet a beauty that is entirely its own. It needs shade and protection from wind. Both the Indian *P. emodi* and its American relative *P. peltatum*, known there as May Apple, have flat-topped lobed leaves about a foot (300mm.) high, and nodding pink flowers like small peonies, which are followed by bantam-egg-sized fruit, equally pink.

POLYGONATUM.   Solomon's Seal is one of the treasures of our own woods, arching over the flowering bluebells with perfect complementary grace.

x **hybridum** ADS   *3 × 1ft (900 × 300mm.)   May*

The produce of two very similar species is the one usually seen in gardens and exhibits suitably hybrid vigour. Although preferring moist shade it will flourish even beneath holm oaks if the humus content of the soil can be built up. Lovely under camellias, which by this time are looking a bit *déjà vu*, with hostas, ferns and smilacina.

There are rare variegated and double-flowered forms and an American monster (*P. commutatum*) reputed to get twice the size, suitably in scale with large-leaved rhododendrons.

POLYGONUM. It is comforting that in addition to knotgrass and other noxious weeds the genus offers some good garden plants as well. It also includes those vast broad-leaved plants with bamboo-like stalks which were so often rashly planted in water gardens in the past. Nonetheless they look lovely and the dead stalks are admirable for Guy Fawkes bonfires, when every node explodes like a pistol shot. Better not plant them, though, unless your acres are broader than most.

amplexicaule   *4 × 4ft (1·2 × 1·2m.)   July–September*

A fine leafy plant with tight sprays of tiny flowers which in 'Atrosangineum' are a definite crimson. A good wild-garden plant or under shrubs though mean in growth in dry soils.

bistorta 'Superbum'   *2 × 2ft (600 × 600mm.)   June–July*

A selected form of our common bistort is a good north-border plant for moist soils.

campanulatum   *3½ × 3ft (1 × 1m.)   July–September*

A very elegant though rather rampageous plant for moist spots. Grey-green foliage and lovely spray of soft heather-bell flowers in cool pink.

polystachyum   *5 × 5ft (1·5 × 1·5m.)   September–October*

A bigger and even more invasive plant with almost spiraea-like heads of white flowers. For woodland glades and big wild garden spots.

PRIMULA. One of the groups which makes every gardener covet water and, failing that, shady spots in which to encourage a range of these beauties to grow. Primroses, of course, are woodland plants par excellence (open hillsides in the Outer Isles, equally covered with them never cease to surprise: their need for moisture at the root and humidity around the leaves is presumably equally met). In the garden they can be encouraged round the boles of trees, and the introduction of a few of the soft pink *P. sibthorpii* will gradually develop into a range of pale shades which may colonize thin grass. Also there are lovely named forms such as 'Garryarde Guinevere' while the double primroses can develop into something of a cult: few are easy to grow. Another annual primula pleasure is polyanthus time and, as may be seen at Sissinghurst, Kent, under hazelnut trees (Kentish Cobs, no doubt) one of the most splendid spectacles the season has to offer. Such a sight, however, as V. Sackville-West demonstrated, is not simply obtained. Plants must be lifted, divided and replanted every year after flowering and the soil encouraged with bonemeal and leafmould if the strain is not to deteriorate. For such general garden effect it is better to eschew the biggest flowering types and use well-tried strains in a restricted range of colours, such as 'Munstead'.

For small borders or north-facing rock beds there are numbers of esoteric Himalayans as well as well-known little garden primulas such as 'Wanda' (if only the sparrows permit).

Bigger, and relishing shade if sunnier borders lack moisture, are *P. denticulata*, the Drumstick primula, available from white through the soft lavender of the type to dark crimson and purples.

The pleasures (and, let it be said, labours) of pond- or stream-margin gardening where swathes of primulas dominate the June scene are bound to be for relatively few gardeners. Nonetheless any leafy soil in the least half-shade which can be kept moist can offer homes to the more robust for floral association with meconopses, and later perhaps certain lilies could continue the show.

The candelabra section offers some lovely plants. These carry their flowers in 5 or 6 distinct whorls up 2 — 3ft (600 — 900mm) high stems which are often mealy. The most robust, and hence safe, species for positions that would not be their first choice include:

bulleyana, a strong orange yellow.

167

japonica naturally a purplish-red but careful selection has produced amongst other named forms 'Miller's Crimson' and 'Postford White'.

prolifera is a fine clear yellow, its whorls of flowers borne on particularly elegant scapes.

pulverulenta is another elegant plant with near purple flowers. The lovely 'Bartley Strain' is pale pink, a perfect colour to blend with its mealy-white stems. The 'Bartley Strain' breeds true.

Another section takes its name from *P. sikkimensis*, a strong grower with yellow flowers in an umbel. The leaves of the robust *P. florindae*, unlike all those so far mentioned, are nearly heart-shaped on long stems and from the rosette mealy stems arise 2ft (600mm.) or more high, each topped with a cascade of pale yellow scented flowers.

Success with any of these will inevitably encourage the growing of other candelabra primula species. They are easily raised from fresh seed, preferably sown as soon as ripe in August: overwintered outside in boxes, one or two might flower the next year but the real display is expected the following year. They are generally not long-lived and it is wise to have a few coming on each year.

Most of us, without the perfect waterside conditions, will not have many of each. Colours, however, must be carefully considered and the fiercer reds or magentas cooled with the foliage of other things.

PRUNELLA vulgaris is our native Self-heal, once considered invaluable for the staunching of haemorrhages. As low ground cover for moist places its blue spikes in summer are welcome. 'Loveliness' is a pink variant.

PULMONARIAS are the lungworts, useful cottage garden plants for early flower and later foliage, whose frequent spots have given both the vernacular and Latin names. Early herbalists saw in spots and leaf shape a certain guide to pulmonary disorders. There are a half dozen of these borage relations sharing with other members the odd, yet charming, habit of opening flowers one colour, usually pink, and turning then blue before falling. This has led to the other common name of Soldiers and Sailors. The following are usually available but any on offer are worth collecting for building up stock sufficient to use for ground cover under spring flowering shrubs such as corylopsis and forsythia.

angustifolia   *1 × 1½ft (300 × 450mm.)   March*

An immaculate (literally) lungwort with good blue flowers from pink buds. There are one or two named forms such as 'Munstead Variety' and 'Sissinghurst White'.

officinalis   *1 × 1½ft (300 × 450mm.)   March*

This is the species with medicinal overtones. Spotted leaves and flowers of conventional colour. For garden use it is less distinctive than the others but still of value.

rubra   *1 × 2ft (300 × 600mm.)   January–March*

Eventually quite a robust plant but the earliest unfolding flowers appear on very short stalks. Their clear coral-red, however, is unique at that season of the year.

saccharata   *1 × 2ft (300 × 600mm.)   March–April*

Perhaps the most vigorous (except *mollis*, seldom available), with greyish spotted leaves and a fine sequence of colour from opening flowers.

RANUNCULUS. Most garden-worthy buttercups are sun-lovers but our three common meadow buttercups — all lovely plants in the right place — have old-established double forms worth searching out. *R. acris* can reach 3 feet (1m.) but *R. bulbosus* and *repens* are only a third of that size. The latter runs about somewhat, especially in moist soil.

aconitifolius *3 × 3ft (1 × 1m.)   April–May*

A lovely white buttercup with generous foliage. The double form here is known as 'Fair Maids of France' and is worth every effort to obtain. For half shade.

REINECKIA carnea is a bit like a small *Liriope* but flowers earlier with spikes of pink. Runs slowly (indeed creeps) in leafy soil.

RHEUM palmatum. Ordinary culinary rhubarb would be a striking enough plant if brought into the border and encouraged to flower but this is better, especially in its 'Atrosanguineum' or 'Bowles's' forms. The deeply divided leaves have purplish reverses and the 6ft (2m.) high flower heads are brightly crimson. Not for deep shade but in dryish soil some is essential.

RODGERSIA. Fine strong plants of a scale to fit with the bigger hostas and Solomon's Seal; they enjoy leafy moist soil. While only the first makes the claim to its name, others also have leaves like those of big horse-chestnuts, each emerging on its own hairy stalk from the ground. The cream or pinkish flowers are rather like scaled-up Meadow Sweet.

aesculifolia *4 × 2ft (1·2m. × 600mm.)   June–July*

The grandest, with purplish-bronze leaves topped by big heads of flower.

pinnata *3 × 2ft (1m. × 600mm.)   June–July*

Here the chestnut-leaves are paired back to back, with straw-berries-and-cream-coloured flowers. 'Superba' is a form that lives up to its name, with bigger, shiny leaves and bright pink flowers.

podophylla   *3 × 3ft (1 × 1m.)   June–July*

On top of their stem the leaflets more resemble a whorl of oak leaves. Unfurling bronze, they green in the fullness of summer but turn dark again in autumn if in sufficient light.

tabularis   *3 × 2½ft (900 × 750mm.)   July*

The leaf shape here takes on quite another form, being circular, almost 3ft (1m.) across, and held up centrally by its stalk, resembling an inflated peltiphyllum (q.v.). Above these trays of pale green the pale cream flowers are held in spikes up to 5ft (1·5m.) A plant of great architectural value in its season but, like any herbaceous plant of its size, leaving a big hole in winter.

SAXIFRAGA. Many of this huge genus are rosette-forming alpine or sub-alpine plants which have no place here but two sections offer valuable shade plants for the front of borders. Firstly the 'mossy' saxifrages. As the name suggests, wide clumps of tight green growth develop and bear thin stalks with relatively large flowers, pink or white. Species included here are *Ss. geranioides, hypnoides* and *trifurcata*.

   A second group is based upon that old favourite London Pride (*S. umbrosa*), whose evergreen rosettes of flat leaves put up such faery stems of pink-spotted white flowers. Excellent ground cover and a May-June display. One clump pulled apart in early autumn will furnish quite an area.

fortunei   *1 × 1ft (300 × 300mm.)   October*

After a high-summer gap without saxifrages this surprising and delightful plant rounds off the year with diffuse heads of white flowers above fine waved leaves. shining green backed with red. 'Wada's Variety' is a form from Japan now available here with even bolder foliage. It must be remembered, however, that the plant turns to jelly at the first hard frost and is not therefore for a cold garden.

SCOPOLIA carniolica ADS   ½ × 1½ft *(150 × 460mm.)*
March–April

Not often seen, this odd potato relation puts up its stems hung with orange-brown bells very early in the season, when it exhibits a definite charm. But it becomes dull later, so plant with other, later, things.

SCROPHULARIA aquatica 'Variegata'   *3 × 1ft (900 ×*
300mm.)

No beauty of flower but the creamy variegated leaves light up a shady border, in moist soil, most effectively.

SENECIO. Ligularias having been botanically separated from Senecio the genus offers little shade-garden value. But, in the north especially, *S. smithii* from the Falkland Islands is good in moist soil. It has pale green, rather dock-like leaves and high heads of creamy white daisies in high summer. The fluffy seed heads remain decorative for many weeks.

SMILACINA racemosa. The False Spikenard. A favourite plant throughout its growth. Arching stems of apple-green leaves produce creamy heads rather like a drooping astilbe (though related to Solomon's Seal). It resents lime and in good leafy soil it will make a wide clump, 2ft (600mm.) high. Like hostas the foliage turns a clear yellow with autumn frosts.

SMYRNIUM. From a genus of a half dozen or so here are a couple of very useful umbellifers

olusatrum   *3 × 2ft (900 × 600mm.)   March–April*

Bright shining green clumps of leaves overwinter and push up heads rather like a smaller Angelica in early spring. It has taken out naturalization papers in the south and south west of England and seems happy in hedge-banks as in cliff-faults. Moisture is required.

perfoliatum ADS   *2½ × 1½ft (760 × 460mm.)   May*

A brilliant spurge-yellow biennial for naturalizing under trees and shrubs. Its time above ground seems very short: at the end of its first year it overwinters by a tuberous root which flowers and dies the following spring. If growing plants can be obtained self-sown seedlings will probably occur: germinating seed one-self seems much more difficult.

SPEIRANTHA gardenii is a lovely little plant like an evergreen Lily of the Valley and with slightly later spikes of starry white flowers. It likes similar conditions but spreads far less rapidly, more's the pity.

STYLOPHORUM diphyllum. A charming North American woodlander attaining 18 in (460mm.) or so. It resembles a smaller-leaved, but bigger-flowered Greater Celandine — just the attributes needed by the latter plant which is apt to be rather weedy.

SYMPHYTUM. Bristly perennial borages, the Comfreys are easily grown and useful plants, but the bigger the coarser.

grandiflorum   *1 × 2ft (300 × 600mm.)   May*

The best for low ground cover, with crosiers of nodding pale yellow flowers in spring. Wide swathes of ground even in dryish shade will be colonized. Erupting clumps of Day Lilies look well as changes in emphasis.

orientale   *2 × 2ft (600 × 600mm.)   May*

Surprisingly soft for a Comfrey, with pale green leaves and profuse white flowers. This and other clump-forming species such as *caucasicum* (blue) and x *uplandicum* (pink changing to blue and 4ft (1·2m. high) should be cut down after flowering, when fresh new leaves will appear to enliven the rest of the season.

TELLIMA   *2 × 1½ft (600 × 460mm.)   May*

grandiflora. Clumps of rounded leaves put up thin spikes of little fringed bells. Ground cover ability under shrubs is good, with the leaves turning bronze in winter. This pleasant trait is emphasized in the form 'Purpurea'. An attractive, easily grown plant, at all seasons.

TIARELLA. Admirable ground cover under shrubs or for the front of shady borders. As with Tellima the leaves turn bronze in winter. White foamy spikes about 9 inches high in *cordifolia* and rather more in *wherryi* hide the foliage in May.

TOLMIEA menziesii. 'Pick-a-back', with old leaves carrying a developing young plant. Rather Tellima-like in leaf but the little flowers on 18 in. (460mm.) spikes are brown and rather dull.

TRACHYSTEMON orientale ADS. Another splendid bristly borage for ground cover on the grandest scale. In February and March the bare soil starts to produce spikes of blue stars whose declining beauty is discreetly hidden by the developing leaves. These by midsummer are huge: excellent under trees in any position.

TRICYRTIS. The oriental Toad Lilies make no dramatic show but always fascinate on closer inspection. For the ideal moist and leafy woodland soil or a suitable synthetic alternative. There are several species, all rather similar, with 2 − 3ft (600 − 900mm.) high spikes of smallish purple-spotted flowers. Elegant and distinctive.

TRIENTALIS europaea is the Chickweed Wintergreen of our northern pinewoods. This charming little plant is well worth introducing into similar garden situations — cool leafy soil in full shade where, if suited, it will run about in an unaggressive way.

TRILLIUM. There are about thirty of these exquisite Wake-robins, related to our Herb Paris but with leaves and floral parts, as the name suggest, in threes. All are worth growing. They appreciate a deep moist leafy soil. While they are admirable in woodland as in their natural habitats they are ideal for that special shady bed where other treasures are nurtured. The species likely to be available include

cernuum   *1½ × 1ft (450 × 300mm.)   April*

The white flower above the leafy triad is carried on a long peduncle and hence is nodding.

erectum   *1½ × 1ft (450 × 300mm.)   April*

Brown-purple flowers above the fine leaves are noticeably foetid, hence the American Common name of 'Stinking Benjamin'. A striking plant but not for near the house.

grandiflorum   *1 − 1½ × 1ft (300 − 460 × 300mm.)   April*

Probably the best 'doer' in our gardens. The flowers are about 3in. (80mm.) across, of perfect whiteness which pinkens as they age. It makes a happy, graceful clump: a favourite plant for dappled shade in leafy soil.

TROLLIUS. The Globe Flowers are plants of moist meadows and hence, in suitable water-retentive soils, enjoy full sun. On light sands, however, full sun makes them wilt piteously; a north-facing border is ideal.

acaulis   *6 × 9in. (150 × 230mm.)   May*

Is one of the dwarf species from the Himalayas with 2-inch wide double buttercup flowers, deep orange and big for the plant. *Pumilus* is related.

x **cultorum**   *2½ × 1½ft (760 × 460mm.)   May*

A trispecific hybrid of which the next species is a part. Several named clones are offered. 'Earliest of All' lives up to its name, flowering in mid April, and 'Goldquelle' is also recommended.

europaeus   *2 × 1½ft (600 × 460mm.)   May*

The true Globe Flower of our cool northern meadows, as well as much of upland Europe. The spherical flowers, above good buttercup foliage, are clear soft yellow. Even more beautiful is the form 'Superbus'.

ledebourii   *2 – 3 × 1½ft (600 – 900 × 460mm.)   May–June*

There is some doubt as to the true name of the plant *T. chinensis* usually offered under this name. Nonetheless it is a good robust Globe Flower with anemone-centred blooms in soft orange. A good, named clone is 'Imperial Orange'.

TROPAEOLUM speciosum. To succeed with this lovely Chilean herbaceous climber is a major feat, but something of an erratic test of one's green-fingeredness. In peaty, moist soil, especially, in the north it scrambles over shrubs with the greatest facility; elsewhere it is often difficult to start and growing pot-plants should always be obtained.

The Flame Flower's great virtue is that, flowering from early June onwards, it brings a second season of colour to things that have otherwise been over for weeks if not months. Great ropes of little scarlet nasturtium flowers are thrown out, often 6 – 8ft (2 – 2·5m.) high, from its supporting host. Growing it through an old yew hedge is another splendid ploy.

UVULARIA. A small group of charming Solomon Seal relations from North America enjoying similar conditions.

grandiflora   *2 × 1ft (600 × 300mm.)   May*

Is the only one likely to be available. It has pale yellow bells with twisted petals hanging from its arched growth. Fleeting in flower it is known in America as Merrybells.

VANCOUVERIA. The three species are like smaller versions of Epimedium, with which they were once botanically joined. Under shrubs they offer similar virtues of elegant leaves which unfold in shades of pink and above which the tiny yellow or white flowers hover like a cloud of flies.
V. hexandra is deciduous, while *Vv. chrysantha* and *planipetala* are evergreen; the latter in California is called Inside-out-Flower.

VERATRUM. One of the most striking herbaceous perennials for shade: above broad, deeply ribbed leaves which make an almost bromeliad-like rosette, great spikes of starry flowers shoot up. They last long in flower and maintain their statuesque effect when this passes, in the green species almost imperceptibly, into seed for several months. Moist shade is enjoyed.

album   *5 × 2ft (1·5m. × 600mm.)   July–August*

Just to confuse it is known as False Helleborine but related neither to Hellebore nor to Helleborine, in fact it is a member of the *Liliaceae*. The great spikes of flower are of palest avocado green.

nigrum   *5 × 2ft (1·5m. × 600mm.)   July*

Here the flowers are of an extraordinary burnished maroon — each spike carries hundreds and makes a remarkable sight for some weeks. Worth every effort to secure.

viride   *4 × 2ft (1·2m. × 600mm.)   July*

This is an American plant (the other two are European) once used as an arrow poison and also in trial by ordeal by the Indians. The highly poisonous alkaloids of all Veratrums slow down the heart — eventually to the point at which it stops. *V. viride*, as its name suggests, is green-flowered, and is another lovely garden plant.

VIOLA. Many violets are plants of woodland or hedgebanks and remain charming for just those roles in the garden. Those needing division are good for the front of shady borders, where they can have an eye kept on them (out of sight is apt to be out of mind until it is too late) while others can be left to seed about under shrubs.

cornuta   *9in. × 1½ft (230 × 460mm.)   May–June*

Long spurred flowers of true deep violet (as they should be) are produced in quantity. This is a parent of the tufted pansies. Mr Thomas recommends clipping over the plants after flowering to encourage the production of a second, early autumn, crop. The evergreen leaves make good ground cover.

hederacea   *6in. × 1ft (150 × 300mm.)   May*

This Australian violet with blue and white flowers held well above the creeping stems may not be generally hardy. A potful can always be overwintered as insurance and is well worth the trouble.

labradorica   *6in. × 1ft (150 × 300mm.)   April–May*

Particularly valuable for its deep purple leaves which a modicum of sun will darken. The flowers are a good light blue. Seeds itself around happily, never becoming a pest.

papilionacea   *9in. × 1ft (230 × 300mm.)   May*

A robust violet from the eastern United States where it is the commonest native species. Various colour forms exist in the wild and in cultivation. It succeeds happily at the boles of trees and would be ideal to give interest to the base of a lawn specimen to follow snowdrops or aconites.

septentrionalis *6 × 6in. (150 × 150mm.) May*

A small plant with outsize flowers, pale blue in the type but the white form available is particularly attractive having a green 'eye' from which purple veining feathers down into the lower petals. This is another North American woodlander, this time from the Appalachian Mountains.

9 Bulbs in the Shade

This chapter is concerned not just with plants whose resting organs are literally bulbs — that is, a collection of swollen and compressed leaf bases upon a flattened basal stem-disc — but other species which disappear below ground for some of the year and re-emerge for their relatively short flowering and leafing season. It has already been shown that such a pattern of growth is typical of many plants directly adapted to woodland conditions and that it has developed in response to light and moisture availability beneath deciduous trees. It provides the main layer of woodland beauty in the spring.

The plants described in this section therefore include, with the true bulbs such as Narcissus and Endymion, tubers such as Cyclamen. Where the plant is relatively large, however, it is listed under herbaceous plants, as are some smaller species grouped under their generic headings, as in Anemone. All are native to woodland areas of Europe, North America and the Himalayan foothills. The range is potentially tremendous but there are the normal problems of availability. Those keen to extend their plant collections in this field should be willing to spend time and patience upon growing the plants on from seed which may be offered more frequently than flowering-sized specimens. There is enormous pleasure in home-raised stock: it may include interesting variants and one starts with a useful number at a not exorbitant cost.

As perennials, one's hope is that bulbous (using the word in its non-botanical, broadest sense) plants will behave thus, going from strength to strength and colonizing shady areas under shrubs or in woodland as they do (or are presumed to do) in their native habitats. An impression of at least apparent naturalism is often important.

Nonetheless it must be agreed that even a shade garden is

not natural, but a highly sophisticated combination of units carefully arranged to develop something of an ecological equilibrium, the balance being maintained, if one is to be honest, by effective gardening. This no doubt is why it is possible to consider gardening an art form.

It permits and even encourages the inclusion here, in all but the most purist circles, of plants which do not really 'belong'. There must, of course, still be some direct connection for the association to be acceptable — for it to look right even when, if deep thought is given to it, it is an ecological impossibility. (Perhaps, indeed, that phrase is itself one definition of a garden. Certainly it sounds like an examination question of daunting complexity. Discuss.)

Thus, although they are not listed separately below, one can add to the scene non-shade lovers such as species tulips and crocuses. The latter in particular must have a reasonable light concentration or the flowers will fail to open (and one of the great pleasures of say, *Crocus chrysanthus*, and its selections is the dusky feathering of colours on the outside of the petals seen when they are closed, compared to the brilliance of their open stars and contrasting stigmata and stamens).

Such plants succeed in visual association because they are, with all bulbs and corms, botanically monocotyledons; and relations, in the plant world at least, usually get on well together. They are most likely, however, to lack that desirable character of permanence, and they often decline to a useless non-flowering state in two or three years. Everyone who grows the lovely little yellow *Iris danfordiae* understands this: the bulbs always break down after flowering. But we still buy it. Used with restraint, this may not matter; the cost is not vast to add annually a few clumps of this or that to brighten a particular spot or to build up an especially felicitous combination at an important focal position.

One further point. Bulbous plants are usually above ground only for the first six months of the year and for the first and last of these are visually no great shakes. What about the rest? Some combination with ground cover is obviously desirable, unless the garden is big enough for the area virtually to be

181

avoided for half the year, or unless in woodland proper the leaf-litter is of such quality as to be attractive in its own right.

Both the herbaceous and shrub lists in this book include suitable ground cover plants for shade but unless they are used only in their own right they should come into their full growth at a time when they are not in serious competition with the bulbs beneath. Winter Aconite, flowering in February and virtually out of sight by May when Lily of the Valley is at its first flush is the sort of pairing to accomplish. Practice and observation will develop others. Now to the bulbs themselves.

ALLIUM. The culinary arts would be utterly at a loss without onions, leeks, shallots, chives and garlic (some people might add 'so much the better' to the last): in the garden, while not so vital, there are some highly ornamental species. Of these without doubt the best are sun-lovers. For our needs, *A. triquetrum* is a valuable plant, making fresh green tufts of leaves in winter above which stems of white, green-striped bells push up at Easter time. It spreads — and has become naturalized in the warmer parts of these islands — but not to the extent that our truly native Ramsons (*A. ursinum*) can take over a woodland floor in moist soil. Visually the effect is stunning brilliant green — the ultimate in Marvel's 'green thought in a green shade', already quoted, but only extreme alliophiles enjoy the smell for long.

Anemone *See* Herbaceous list
Arisaema *See* Herbaceous list
Arisarum *See* Herbaceous list
Arum *See* Herbaceous list

CYCLAMEN. Hardy cyclamen are one of the joys of the garden. It is impossible to have too many and with a collection of the dozen or so species available flowers are possible for most of the year: for shade we can use *C. coum* and its forms. For a carefully selected spot under a choice shrub — *Corylopsis* perhaps or *Corylus avellana* 'Contorta' — where their cowslip yellow waves above the chubby pink and purple cyclamen flowers. When happy this little plant will seed itself around and appear in a surprising range of places.

hederifolium (neapolitanum) ADS. An extraordinarily nonchalant species from southern Europe. It produces its exquisite shuttlecock flowers, pink or white, from rock-hard ground in August and continues into October. As the swelling seed capsules wind down to soil level on spring-like stalks the developing leaves, marbled green and grey, start to provide a winter-long carpet of quiet colour; attractive until May.

This is one of the few plants that one might put — with a clump or two of *Galanthus elwesii* and *Iris foetidissima* — at the base of an important specimen lawn tree — just enough apart from each other to supply a few weeks of added interest where the bole meets the soil.

repandum. A woodland species with good marbled leaves and deep rose-pink flowers in May. Less easy to establish than the others.

All cyclamen, if bought as dry corms, should be planted with a bit of peat or leaf litter and with the smooth side down. Better is to obtain pot-grown plants in leaf or, indeed and, grow one's own from seed. Flowering takes two to three years.

ENDYMION. Our common English bluebell has gone through so many names that one can choose erratically from almost a dozen. (It is now at *Hyacinthoides non-scriptus*.) It is of course a classic woodland plant to be encouraged if one has it, to be obtained if not. But for the garden the Spanish bluebell, *E. hispanicus*, is a better bet, being more tolerant of drier spots under shrubs. It is available in a wide range of soft colours from white, through pink to blue, and seeds itself around happily.

ERANTHIS. The Winter Aconite, each golden buttercup-like flower surrounded by a choirboy's ruff of green, is one of the most heartening signs of earliest spring. In moist limy or lime-free woodland it carpets the ground, spreading out into grass.

183

But it is resentful of cultivation above it and difficult to establish from dry tubers, as usually offered, unless bought in quantity with the expectation of a 50 per cent failure rate. One nursery at least offers pot-grown plants in leaf in spring, more expensive but much more certain.

hyemalis is the usual, naturalized aconite: *E. cilicica* and the bispecific hybrid between the two (x *tubergenii*) have rather bigger flowers of greater substance.

ERYTHRONIUM. The lovely woodlilies from North America are seldom seen to much effect here. This is sad because they are amongst the very best things which that very rich flora can offer. Our European counterpart *E. dens-canis* (Dog's-tooth Violet — a fool name: it is not at all violet-like and the canine-tooth bit refers to the tubers, well out of sight) is equally beautiful in a restrained sort of way. Of the Americans *E. revolutum* 'White Beauty' and *E. oregonum* are generally available. Those from further South (*E. californicum* and *E. tuolumnense*) like more sun. Lime-free leaf mould is appreciated.

GALANTHUS. A woodland garden, or indeed any garden, without snowdrops hardly deserves the name. Flower is possible from October through to March but the pre-Christmas species from Greece need more sun than woodland gives them and need not be considered here. Of the rest *G. nivalis* is our native snowdrop, which has produced a range of variants whose most miniscule differences have been pounced upon with glad cries by galanthomaniacs. These often kind people are apt to pass on the disease with generous gifts of the plants which spread it: there is no known antidote.

The wild snowdrop increases freely in both its common double and single forms in moist woodland or under shrubs where cultivations are eschewed. Where the broad effect is impossible clumps of the bigger selected types are better: 'Magnet', 'Atkinsii', or 'Sam Arnott' for instance. Their cost, however, may surprise the unprepared.

Other good species from south-east Europe prefer drier soil but still enjoy shade; they include *G. caucasicus* and the bright green-leaved *G. platyphyllus* (*ikariae latifolius*).

Like Cyclamen, snowdrops are best bought growing 'in the green' as it is described and any moving done at home should be carried out as soon as flowering is over. Feeding snowdrops with bonemeal at this time and division of tight clumps every three or four years pays dividends.

LEUCOJUM The snowflakes are less well known.

aestivum. The so-called Summer Snowflake in fact flowers in April but its lush clumps of daffodil-like leaves make it conspicuous from Christmas onward. It is native to willow-shaded damp meadows but seems remarkably amenable to drier spots so long as it is protected from the sun. 'Gravetye' is a superior form.

vernum. Enjoys moist shade and flowers with the snowdrops. Here all six perianth segments are the same size, making a regular bell-form, white with yellow tips.

LILIUM. Most lilies are rather like Clematis in that they appreciate shade at the roots but enjoy bringing their heads into the sun. That, too, is how they look best: sun, especially dappled sun, adds brilliance and a crystalline dimension to the petals.

It is not surprising that, like roses, certain lilies have been cultivated as objects of beauty, and also for use in religious celebrations, since earliest times. The Madonna Lily shares with the rose the role of beauty's epitome.

There are some 80 wild species of lilies spread around the northern hemisphere. They differ so greatly in form and in cultivational requirements that it is not easy to devise any useful groupings. To some extent perhaps a simple geographical classification is a help, if only as an aide-memoire. Unlike daffodils, hyacinths or tulips, the bulbs of lilies are without an enclosing tunic, being made up of overlapping scales like a loose globe artichoke. They thus desiccate quickly when out of the soil: also roots never fully dry up at the resting time. 'Shelf-life' at a plant centre is thus distinctly limited.

Britain has no native lily but, in places *L. martagon* and *L. pryenaicum* (deep purple or white and yellow respectively) have become naturalized. To see the former in the wood at St John's College, Cambridge, is to realize how good it can be in light deciduous shade. Association with foxgloves and *Campanula lactiflora* is superb.

L. pyrenaicum is a smaller plant, but another Turk's Cap as are most Europeans. It is often seen as one of the few garden plants remaining around a ruined Highland croft. In the south, especially in dry light soil it succeeds in full shade. Other fine Turk's Caps are the tall *L. szovitsianum* and *L.* x *testaceum*.

The lovely Madonna Lily, *L. candidum*, is a mysterious plant of highly erratic preferences. Often seen best in cottage gardens in full sun in a row in the vegetable garden, at Highdown near Worthing, Sussex, it succeeded best in shade — perhaps slightly embarrassed by the grand company it kept there. Usually, like the other Europeans, it prefers lime — but then one will see successful groups in acid soil in Scotland. It is all very confusing: if good stock can be obtained one must just experiment. It is worth every effort. One thing is certain, coming into growth in late summer and with overwintering leaves it must be planted in August at the latest: other lilies are best moved in October.

While North America has several Turk's Cap lilies a more typical flower shape is that of long nodding bells, elegantly held. In general they are less easy to grow here. A gritty soil with plenty of leafmould helps and adequate summer moisture is important. *L. pardalinum*, a tall scarlet Turk's Cap is known sometimes to grow in water, but *running* water, in its Californian home. Moisture is thus highly necessary, but bad drainage is anathema.

From the Orient come our commonest, and generally easiest, garden lilies. While the Europeans have been in cultivation with us since mediaeval times and many of the Americans since the eighteenth century (John Bartram first sent the lovely

L. superbum, to Peter Collinson in the 1730s), most orientals are of more recent origin. Surprisingly, with their consciousness of floral beauty, the Chinese used lilies more for food than for garden decoration.

In general they are plants for open glades in woodland or amongst shrubs, which give young growth some frost protection (the resting bulbs are rock-hardy). Deep shade causes etiolated shoots, poor flowers and lack of permanence. The easiest of all, *L. regale,* really must have its head in sun, but the similar *L. leucanthum* also with fine white trumpets, takes more shade. So, too, does the Turk's Cap, *L. henryi* whose soft orange petals bleach in full sun.

While happy to have at least half shade several of the bigger lilies — the golden-rayed lily of Japan (*L. auratum*) for example — also appreciate wind protection afforded by woodland. This is especially so of the giant Himalayan lily, now moved into a genus of its own, *Cardiocrinum*. This marvellous monster, 10ft (3m.) high with up to 20 long white flowers held as do the angels their trumpets on the organ in King's College Chapel, is one of the most dramatic plants a moist woodland glade can grow. Bulbs take several years to build up to flowering size and are then monocarpic. Anyone with the space is bound to try it.

With such a wealth of species hybridists have worked busily upon lilies and in many cases hybrid vigour has produced excellent garden plants. Catalogues must be consulted: 'Bellingham Hybrids' offer tall Turk's Caps, 'Aurelian Hybrids' have wide-flaring trumpets in shades of soft apricot and orange. 'African Queen' and 'Golden Splendour' strains have *regale*-shaped flowers in a range of colours. 'Creelman Hybrids' are an improvement upon that species itself. 'Harlequin Hybrids' are again Turk's Caps but, with the Chinese *L. willmottiae* in their parentage are very light and graceful in effect. With careful choice, sufficient space and a deep enough pocket lilies may be had in flower from June to October inclusive.

MUSCARI. Even the commonest Grape Hyacinth is not a plant for deep shade. There, the already long leaves become etiolated and the flower spikes reduce proportionately. Yet on the edge of shrub plantings they can be a great success. Leafing begins as early as September, while the clear blue flowers do not follow until April. They increase easily.

NARCISSUS. If there is one plant that needs no description it is Narcissus. Daffodils, beloved by all, flower in every garden from windowbox to stately home and are grown by the acre as cut flowers for several months on end. Only their diversity and use need comment here.

There are between 20 and 30 wild species of Narcissus, spread about Europe and extending into North Africa. Several interbreed in the wild and in cultivation the genus has been the subject of intense hybridization: many hundreds of resultant cultivars have been named.

With such a wide natural distribution it is obvious that not all are suitable for our general needs in the shady garden. Fortunately *Narcissus pseudonarcissus* is the lovely little Lent Lily of deciduous woodlands of southern England and France. It is the typical daffodil and a parent of the majority of later forms. Several closely related species and primary hybrids such as the old *N.* x *incomparabilis* (with *N. poeticus*) named by Philip Miller in the mid eighteenth century, are entirely suitable.

Following these, over the last two centuries, diversity of shape, length of trumpet (or none — the old cottage garden double yellow is illustrated in Gerard's Herbal of 1597 and with a whole page of forms in Parkinson's *Paradisus* thirty years later) colour and size have been sought. In general all are happy in the part shade of shrubs and deciduous trees and in old orchard grass. Benefitting noticeably from application of a foliar feed to the leaves after flowering they go from strength to strength year after year. There are few more beautiful sights than naturalized daffodils under the soft pink and white of apple trees in flower. The effect appears utterly uncontrived and natural, as indeed it should.

In spite of this, choice of cultivar needs a moment's thought. In the search for further diversity hybridists have brought in colours which though exquisite in themselves no longer associate so easily in the woodland garden. Those with vivid orange and scarlet cups should be kept away from the blue-pink rhododendrons and heathers flowering at the same time; palest yellows and creams are the choice here. Similarly in small gardens the biggest trumpet cultivars are best replaced by smaller, lighter forms, which usually have a bit of *N. cyclamineus* or *N. triandrus* in them: 'February Gold', 'Peeping Tom', and 'Thalia' are fine examples. For garden effect it is always better to plant numbers, relative to the area concerned, of few types rather than a kaleidoscopic mixture of many.

Of the true species one or two have particular roles. The lovely and distinct cyclamen-flowered daffodil enjoys moisture more than most; it has naturalized in wet spots under oaks as well as in open meadow at the Savill Garden in Windsor Great Park: massed around *Rhododendron* x *praecox* the effect it is dramatic.

The little *N. asturiensis* (a perfect daffodil 4in. (100mm.) high) and the hoop-petticoat types (*N. bulbocodium*) are also from Spain and Portugal but need better drainage; they make excellent accompaniment in the garden, as in the wild, with maquis-type shrubs such as brooms and cistus, as do any other of the southern Europeans that can be obtained.

It might just be mentioned in passing that bargain offers 'for naturalizing' of daffodil bulbs which have been forced for flower are just those least able to cope with the competition of orchard grass. If they are to be bought, and bargains are as irresistible as temptations, they should be planted in nursery rows for a year or two to build up strength and size.

10 Ferns for Shade

It would not be an exaggeration to add a word to that phrase and write 'Ferns *are* for shade'. This is quite true; mainly because ferns are, by comparison with all the other plants discussed in this book, evolutionarily more primitive. They are nearer the beginning of that classic struggle in which starting with simple algae in water hundreds of millions of years ago, the plant kingdom began to colonize dry land. Gradually more highly developed plants evolved: ancestors of mosses and liverworts first and eventually the flowering plants as we know them, each group and each species perfectly adapted — as we have seen with regard to shade — to a particular ecological niche.

Evolutionarily, it seems that ferns take a place between the Thallophytes (mosses and liverworts) and the Spermatophytes, the seed-bearing plants, their closest relationships perhaps being with conifers and cycads, the simplest Spermatophytes. The full group is know as Pteridophytes, and includes not just recognizable ferns but fern-allies — the Selaginellas, Club-mosses and Equisetums. None of these are likely to be chosen as garden plants: the last named are the horsetails, often extremely persistent noxious weeds. (This is a pity: *E. telmateia*, the greater horsetail, is an extremely beautiful plant for moist shade but runs for miles underground and becomes completely out of control.)

The point that is being made about the relatively primitive origin of ferns is that in becoming able to succeed in drier and drier conditions plants have had to develop organs and techniques to avoid desiccation. One such development is a cuticle of varying thickness on the, usually, upper surfaces of leaves which prevents or helps to reduce water loss. This is, of course, especially necessary for plants growing in full sun. Ferns have a less developed cuticle. Although in evolutionary terms they have come a long way from algae, and, with their highly effective conducting tissues not far short of conifers, have gone a long way towards the seed-bearing plants, ferns are still very dependent upon moisture.

This dependence is double-edged. Lack of a fully effective cuticle means that even mature fern plants dry up and die more quickly if sufficient moisture is not available from the soil: it also means that atmosphere humidity is important and that, in turn, means shade as a desideratum of successful cultivation.

There is another aspect in which ferns are utterly moisture-dependent and this is in reproduction. In the garden we are usually happy to increase ferns by division, which is just as well because their sexual method is a decidedly complicated one.

Ferns, we observe, do not flower but bear, usually under their fronds (leaves), bars or spots of darker tissue which eventually produce dust-like spores (lay a mature fern frond on white paper overnight and a perfect pattern of the spore-producing sori is reproduced by next morning). If spores are sown a new fern plant does not develop, for these are not seeds, product of sexual fusion. Germination of a spore in moisture and shade produces a tiny liverwort-like plate of green tissue, the prothallus. This in turn eventually develops male and female sexual organs and motile spermatozoids from the former swim to fertilize the latter. Only now does a first little recognizable fern frond develop as a start towards the plant we know and wish to grow. This pattern of a leafy asexual plant and tiny sexual prothallus is known as the 'alternation of generations'.

The significance of all this is obvious: ferns are very moisture dependent. Ferns are for shade. Throughout the world there are around 10,000 different species of ferns with their greatest concentration in the forested montane areas of the humid tropics. Here they are often epiphytic. In temperate areas wild ferns are usually terrestrial, but still woodland plants. (Bracken is a fine open-ground exception but no one is likely to recommend it for garden cultivation.) The visual range is considerable: some are deciduous, others evergreen; all are elegant in pattern — 'ferny', 'fern-like' are frequent and very clear adjectives that we use about many other plants, so it should be emphasized that 'Asparagus Fern' is certainly not a true fern.

In spite of this obvious emphasis upon moisture, a few worthwhile species can succeed in dry shade. (The smallest ferns like wall-rue and rusty-back, however, which colonize rock crevices and can retire into a state of semi-quiescence in dry periods, are not listed here though they are charming for rock-gardens.) Both the Lady Fern and Male Fern will take dry shade during summer. But it is important that they have had adequate moisture in spring when their fronds are developing. Without this, though the plants survive, growth is apt to be stunted and the plants lack that essential air of green well-being which is so important a part of their beauty.

In the following select list only those ferns likely to be available from the trade are included though there is no doubt that many good plants, especially from Japan and New Zealand's South Island, have yet to be introduced. Similarly, though a few are still offered, mention is made here only in passing of the mutant forms with cristate or differently divided fronds which were once so keenly collected. The phrase 'The Victorian Fern Craze' (using David Allen's book-title) admirably sums up the intense interest in fern-growing in the middle years of the last century, when the search for variants became an avid occupation especially it seems for reverend gentlemen and ladies of gentle birth. Moore and Lindley's great folio tome of British Ferns (1854) describes in detail 17 common polypody and the 14 male fern types and exquisitely illustrates most of them. The majority of these are now lost to us yet, no doubt, a renaissance in pteridomania would find replacements.

Meanwhile, here are some basic species.

ADIANTUM. Of 200 lovely Maidenhair Ferns strewn about the world only one is native to Europe, spreading north as far as the coasts of our south-western counties. This is

capillus-veneris   *1 × 1ft (300 × 300mm.)*

A typically delicate plant for the sort of sheltered shady nook which suits *Begonia evansiana* (q.v.). Such a combination in a courtyard corner gives the impression of a Wardian case with the lid off.

pedatum   *1½ × 1ft (450 × 300mm.)*

Longer, narrower pinnae, pink when young, on wiry black stems. Another lovely plant for a sheltered spot. The adiantums are delicate plants, both in appearance and in constitution and cannot take much competition from more robust things.

ASPLENIUM scolopendrium. Our native Hart's Tongue fern is one of the most striking foliage plants for shade. To see it lining the steep banks of a sunken Devon lane is to realize its ornamental value. The long evergreen leaves growing in a shuttlecock are barred with sori on the reverse like a mackerel's back. Sufficiently vigorous in moist shade to compete and contrast with hostas and astilbes yet, unlike them, also offering good winter effect.

ATHYRIUM filix-foemina. The Lady Fern of our woodlands is a distinguished plant. Not unlike the Male Fern (q.v. below) but, as its pre-women's lib name suggests, is more elegant, lace-like and altogether more desirable.

goeringianum pictum, the Japanese Painted Fern is a related species of extraordinary beauty: though capable of attaining the Lady Fern's 2ft (600mm.) or so it is apt to be less. The delicate fronds are truly silver flushed with the dark-pink colour of the midribs. This is a plant to build a small garden picture around, arranging that it gets a gleam of late sun, though in moist shade for the rest of the day.

BLECHNUM chilense is one of the biggest ferns we can grow, though, as its country of origin would suggest, it is not for cold areas. In moist shade in the west the evergreen yard-long fronds, like a giant polypody, march strongly across a glade. Our own native Hard Fern, *Blechnum spicant* is less than half the size but highly distinctive in pattern. The open shuttlecock of shining evergreen leaves is topped by taller, thinner fertile fronds.

CYRTOMIUM falcatum. A prized darling of the nineteenth-century ferneries, the Japanese Holly Fern is effective outside only in the milder areas but well worth trying. Half success, or mere survival, is not enough: its beauty lies in the glistening fronds, cut into holly-like sprays.

CYSTOPTERIS bulbifera. A pretty little running fern with pale fronds. Good under small rhododendrons with purple prunella and other small ground-huggers.

DICKSONIA antarctica is the only tree-fern (an Australian) hardy enough for British mainland gardens (though Tresco Abbey garden in the Isles of Scilly, of course, manages others) and then only in the west. It is a plant of the biggest scale for sheltered woodland dells, where its huge 10-foot-wide cart-wheel of fronds is gradually taken to the same height on a trunk of compressed roots. Tree ferns need extremely careful siting if the effect is not to be merely bizarre: where, however, it works a prime spring pleasure is to gaze upward through the unfolding whorl of soft green and see the filigree in unlikely profile against the sky.

DRYOPTERIS. A big genus of confusing origins and nomenclature offering several lovely garden plants.

aemula is the Hay-scented Buckler Fern — the fragrance develops as the fronds fade — with finely dissected fronds some 2 feet high.

dilatata. Darker in colour and more spreading in habit, this is a similar sized plant.

felix-mas ADS. Here is a species which seems to accept that which, for ferns, is the generally unacceptable — dry shade. Certainly the fronds are finer in good conditions but, so long as a reasonable start is given in spring to the first flush of growth, it will maintain itself in remarkably good heart throughout the summer. A common but very worthwhile plant, lovely with foxgloves in a woodland glade.

wallichiana. Mr Graham Thomas describes this Oriental as 'one of the most magnificent of all hardy plants', which, it might be thought, is a compliment not easily lived up to. But the sheaves of unfolding fronds (bent like a scorpion's tail about to strike) green-gold with dark cinnamon midribs are truly magnificent especially when, in good conditions of moist half-shade, mature fronds attain 5ft (1 · 5m.) or so. This is a fern on the grand scale.

MATTEUCIA struthiopteris. The ostrich plume fern is native to Europe and Asia (the American *M. pennsylvanica* is very similar but possibly more upright in growth). It is one of the most lovely ferns for moist shade, with its fresh green shuttle-cocks in spring. These darken with the summer, browning pleasantly in autumn and leaving, for winter effect, the dark velvet fertile fronds standing stiffly erect until the following spring starts the cycle again. Height with us is usually towards 2 feet but it may exceed this if happy.

ONOCLEA sensibilis. The name Sensitive Fern leads the hopeful to expect the waved pale-green fronds to collapse at the touch of a finger like the leaves of *Mimosa pudica*. Sadly, the only fingers to be effective are those of Jack Frost whose lightest breath is enough to send the plant to rest for the winter. When really happy in moist woodland Onoclea reaches 2½ feet and can be quite invasive, but beautifully so.

OSMUNDA regalis. The Royal Fern, still wild in some peaty bog edges in Britain, is by far our most striking native fern. Huge fibrous rootstocks eventually build up, from which unfold the doubly pinnate fronds, fawn-pink when young. Eventually attaining towards 6 feet the topmost pinnae become fertile and look rather like plume poppy. A pool edge is the best spot for success.

POLYPODIUM vulgare. Polypody is the only British fern commonly to behave — at least in moist areas — epiphytically, like so many tropical species. Seen, especially in winter, clothing the upper sides of old oak branches the effect is peculiarly unlikely, un-British indeed. But the leathery evergreen fronds also make admirable if more conventional ground cover. There used to be many crested forms and other oddities, still worth growing if ever offered.

POLYSTICHUM. The shield ferns are some of the loveliest ferns we can grow and certainly the best of the evergreen species.

acrosticoides and **munitum** are from the east and west of North America respectively and known there as Christmas Ferns. The latter is bigger and better — lovely with snowdrops clustering around its base.

Europe's shield ferns are hardly less beautiful and certainly more easily grown. *P. setiferum* survives in old cottage gardens when almost everything else — often the cottage itself — has been overwhelmed with willowherb and brambles. Widespreading, soft-scale-covered fronds are beautiful from the moment they unfold until the following year's growth replaces them: lovely against steps. Some forms bear bulbils and a pegged-down frond roots along its length to make increase easy: often the bulbil types are more divided in the leaf and are particularly fine. They should be sought out. They are wider than high, 2 × 3ft (600 × 900mm.) perhaps.

THELYPTERIS palustris is the marsh fern. Bright yet pale green fronds appear from a running (but not aggressive) rootstock: it is good in moist soil under calcifuge shrubs.

WOODWARDIA radicans. These lists have, intentionally, included quite a number of plants whose reputation for frost hardiness is rightly open to doubt, but given woodland shade are often surprisingly successful. It is suitable therefore that the last should be one such: a lovely big fern with long (up to 5ft (1·5mm.)) arching fronds which root at their tips and gently leapfrog across a sheltered woodland glade. A lovely plant with which to end.

11 The Shaded Garden Throughout the Year

This final chapter is bound to be something of a recapitulation, to act both as an encouragement and as an aide memoire. It is concerned in particular to emphasize the year-long pleasure that a shady garden can provide to the thoughtful owner. In many ways it is sensible to conceive of one's garden in terms of a continuous performance rather than as a series of still views, however spectacular. The analogy is, or ought to be, closer to the Windmill Theatre's proud boast 'We never closed' rather than the penny-in-the slot 'What the Butler Saw' machine slowed down to reveal each part of the composite picture.

It is a continuum, as plants coming to their best succeed each other yet overlap; the declining beauty of one being masked by the ascendency of another. Sometimes the masking is actual, as one plants butterfly gladioli perhaps with flag irises to give summer interest to a spot whose zenith is otherwise passed in June. (Gertrude Jekyll went to enormous effort to achieve this effect, tying plants forward over their predecessors and even plunging pots of maturing things to avoid a gap; but then she had staff.) Sometimes it is almost like sleight of hand to encourage the eye to move quickly on to the plant of the moment.

Yet most plants, at least those grown in situ (as distinct from the bank of potted hydrangeas in full flower hurriedly brought in for a summer wedding or whatever) are not beautiful merely when at their most floriferous. Much of the pleasure we derive from our gardens comes from observing the reactions of our plants to the unfolding seasons; the swelling buds, the lengthening stems, the fragility of the new leaves.

Sometimes, indeed, it seems that, such is the power of anticipation, flowers of even the most beautiful of plants can be almost anticlimatic (*Paeonia mlokosewitschii* in a windy April is

198

a case in point after the build-up the developing leaves have given it). The anticipatory excitement of birthdays and Christmas to children is very similar in effect; the day itself has to be pretty good to live up to its promise. Also, it seems, gardeners have an innate compulsion, of which this anticipation is no doubt a part, to look into the future. Certainly 'You should have seen my garden yesterday' (or last week/month/year) is a common cri-de-coeur, when visitors insist on appearing just as the delphiniums have gone over. But more important to us is what is to come; the planning, ordering, planting now for the pleasures of the next year or even the next decade. Deferred gratification is a recent concept of academic sociologists, apparently deep with significance of class divisions and behaviour; it has been a fact of life for every gardener since Adam. (Perhaps, thinking carefully, those social scientists could apply their theories to those who sow radishes and those who sow acorns.)

NOVEMBER. Thus, in considering the Year in the Shade Garden it seems right to start not at the beginning of a calendar year but in late autumn — that limbo eulogized by one poet as an idyllic 'season of mists and mellow fruitfulness' and by another as the nadir of everything. Some lines of Thomas Hood's 'November' are worth repeating in order, subsequently, to give the lie to what is still apt to be received and accepted wisdom.

> No sun — no moon!
> No morn — no noon
> No dawn — no dusk — no proper time of day.
> No warmth, no cheerfulness, no healthful ease,
> No comfortable feel in any member —
> No shade, no shine, no butterflies, no bees,
> No fruits, no flowers, no leaves, no birds, —
> November.

What actually does November hold for the shade garden? No flowers? Nonsense!

Although we are moving towards the shortest day of the Year and the longest daily period of darkness this is also a time of release and, paradoxically, of lightening for by mid-month almost every deciduous tree has taken on its bare winter aspect and the shade-tolerant species beneath see the sky for the first time in months. Obviously, frost-tender growth of herbaceous plants is cut, becoming brown and sere, here as in the open. There will be little bright autumn leaf-colour as such, for this sunny summer ripening of wood and leaf is an essential pre-requisite; but hostas and smilacina foliage turn clear yellow before degenerating into mush.

More importantly the shiny leaves of evergreen shrubs gleam and sparkle in their new-found light. Those of *Skimmia japonica* frame the sealing-wax berries, those of camellias, ('Forest Green' is especially noteworthy) support the great fat flower buds full of springtime promise and narrow-leaved Aucuba, its berries still green, picks up every fleck of light.

Those few variegated-leaved plants which are happy in shade also come into their own; Aucuba again, of course, Elaeagnus, *Iris foetidissima variegata*, and, of enormous importance, the ivies. Used on the shadiest of walls or as ground cover under trees their value is unrivalled. Such ever-greens have a year-round garden role. They are always there for background, windbreak, cutting for the house, so much indeed that they are apt to become, like well-loved but over-familiar pictures indoors, virtually unconsidered. Then, to extend the simile, as if one has installed new spotlights over the paintings, low winter sun now reaches these plants and they light up in exactly this way. Their character is dramatically altered.

One can forgive Thomas Hood his November dirge because not only did he live in a time of winter fogs of an inevitability and thickness now inconceivable (thanks to modern concern for atmospheric cleanliness) but so many of the plants now avail-able to lighten our darkness, in the Prayerbook's phrase, had not been introduced to European gardens. Or, if here, garden fashion in the first decade of the last century clouded their potential.

November, then, is not merely a time for foliage but also one for flower. Many of those species recommended for winter-flowering are now in their first, and often most spectacular, flush of blossom. Photoperiodic response to day-length and to low temperatures brings them out but, in most years, those frosts hard enough to blacken the dahlias have done no harm to hardier things. Hence *Viburnum* x *bodnantense* is now studded with apple-blossom pink and white. Above, the winter cherry is a cloud of white.

That best of all winter-flowering shrubs, *Mahonia japonica*, will have opened the first primrose yellow bells in October but now there are enough to make a show; it will continue to do so until March or April. In November it is joined by the more florally spectacular *M. lomariifolia* and the *M.* x *media* types such as 'Charity' and 'Buckland'. These splendid plants with their great shuttlecocks of bright yellow give the lie to the canard that winter-flowering plants are shy, retiring little things. Though their flowering season is relatively short by comparison with *M. japonica* — a mere six weeks or so — it is twice that of most summer shrubs.

DECEMBER. As the days shorten still further and move into December we begin to look for plants associated with Christmas itself. 'The Holly and the Ivy, when they are both full grown . . . ' might well be the start to a description of the shade garden as the first line to a well-known carol. Christmas roses, *Helleborus niger*, on the other hand are apt to fail us for some weeks to come. Nonetheless, other hellebores offer far more in garden value. *H. corsicus (H. lividus ssp. corsicus)* is now unfurling its lime-green heads above dramatic rosettes of leaves and the first of the deciduous kinds, *H. atrorubens*, opens the first of its nodding, wine-dark cups.

The traditional walk round the garden on Christmas morning produces, in most years, an amazing number of plants in flower, from last roses to daisies on the lawn. Many appear from the shady garden.

JANUARY. In no time, it seems, we notice or affect to notice that 'the days are really drawing out' as January begins. It has already been described how this season is a vital one for herbaceous plants which are adapted to woodland conditions so

201

that they can get ahead with their life cycle before the summer leaf canopy closes over, making life above ground untenable for them.

Now, therefore, a close examination of the shade garden will show (unless snow covers all) an amazing amount of precocious growth. Narcissus shoots are spearing through the ground, as are bluebells; honeysuckle is showing rosettes of new leaves.

FEBRUARY. The unpredictable nature of a British winter makes it certain that we can never be dogmatic about what is to come — long-range forecasts or no. February can be a brutish month. Often it holds the hardest frosts of all and produces the most snow. Yet a reduction of dark hours offers hope of better things and the strength of the sun — should it deign to shine — is clearly increasing.

In the garden all the winter-flowering shrubs continue. Spidery flowers of witch hazels, opening first just after Christmas, seem virtually impervious to frost, as are those of winter heather. Winter cherry and winter Viburnums put out further flushes in every mild spell while to prove that better things are to come a camellia or two and the first Rhododendrons foolishly appear.

At ground level it is clear that February is the month of snowdrops, of green-ruffed golden aconites and despite its name, at last the Christmas Rose. The Lenten Roses, sumptuous bowls of grape-bloomed plum purple, begin their ten week season.

MARCH. In the shade garden, in all but the most unpleasant years, spring really does get under way in March; the protection afforded by the shade-producers, whether walls or trees, permits the shade-acceptors to unfurl leaves and open flowers. Bergenias are well out, Peonies develop fast, Primula 'Wanda' and the first Epimediums open deep down amongst the browning leaves of last year, which will have to be removed at once. The yellow daisies of *Doronicum* echo the predominant March colour produced by Narcissus and Forsythia. *Daphne odora* is now well out, every shoot tip bearing a cluster of exquisitely scented crystalline flowers. Camellias or, on limy soils, the Japanese Quinces offer richer colours. Rhododendrons are now getting into their stride to become the mainstay of gardens on acid soils for the next three months, often providing the most brilliant display of the year.

APRIL. As April moves forward the herbaceous layer in the shade garden begins its annual task of masking the soil entirely; Foam flower (*Tiarella*), *Tellima, Euphorbia robbiae* and Sweet Cicely spread under the shrub layer now in flower; magnolias, Corylopsis, bridal-wreath spiraeas and brilliant orange barberries.

MAY. It is not merely to fit in with the social season that that great annual feast of flowers, the Chelsea Flower Show, takes place in the first week of May. Now and into June all gardens are, or ought to be, at their very best. The shady site and the woodland garden are no exception, for spring and summer meet at this moment, and with incredible prodigality offer the best of both. Beneath our feet are bluebells and Solomon's Seal, Smilacina and Lily of the Valley; literally dozens of shrubs may be had in flower; *Clematis montana* and honeysuckle hang in swags from the trees or clothe walls.

JUNE. In June, too, the profusion of flower on cotoneasters and pyracanthas indicates the show of berries to follow in autumn. Gardens with that most desirable advantage of moist shade under high oak woodland now have their swathes of candelabra primulas and Himalayan poppies, hardy orchids and geraniums.

JULY. In natural woodland the foliage canopy will have quite closed over by July and the leaves of many of the herbaceous things beneath are yellowing as perforce they begin their high-summer rest. Owners of large gardens, of which woodland is but one part, can possibly accept the apparently inevitable and turn their interest and their visitors' footsteps to other parts.

But for most shade-gardeners space is too limited to be able to behave in so cavalier a manner. And, as previous chapters in this book have shown, it is perfectly possible to continue the interest.

Shrubs, in particular, are no problem and many continue their show for many weeks. Hoherias and hypericums are in the open, and on shady walls hybrid big-flowered Clematis share the space with *Lonicera tragophylla* and the invaluable self-clinging *Hydrangea petiolaris*.

Below, a brilliant green ground cover is maintained by the diversity of fern fronds and hostas, from which emerge lilies, *Campanula lactiflora* and the stiffer *C. latifolia*.

AUGUST. On acid soils it has been possible to find rhododendrons to flower every month of the year so far; August is no exception if space can be found for the magnificent white *R. auriculatum* or 'Polar Bear', a hybrid from it. Just as desirable, but less choosy as to position is *Eucryphia* x *nymanensis*, the best and easiest of its tribe. The pinks, blues and purples of hydrangeas, mop-head and lacecap, are on every side. Sheltered walls offer sites for those highly desirable chileans, Berberidopsis and Lapageria; both continue well into the following month.

SEPTEMBER. September is the central month for fuchsias; high bushes of the small-flowered *F. magellanica* and crinoline-skirted hybrids often behaving as if they were herbaceous. Similar colours are repeated by *Leycesteria formosa* now in both fruit and flower, and by *Hebe* 'Autumn Glory'. Brilliant blue willow gentiana is also now at its best. So too is the unique Kirengeshoma, cool pale yellow.

OCTOBER. It is usually possible to pretend that September belongs, although only just, to summer. As October comes in the acceptance of the circling year becomes inevitable. Many summer plants retain their flowers but the profusion of fruits ripening in a range of colours indicates a culmination of the efforts of the year. This is what the busy flowering of the previous months has all been for — not just to provide a Roman holiday for the bees or an aesthetic experience for humans. Yet, such is our good fortune to enjoy an oceanic climate without extremes of anything, that the seasons imperceptibly merge. October has its own delights — ivory white heads of Fatsia, purple bowls of Colchicums and true autumn crocuses, delicate *Saxifraga fortunei*. But if depression sets in at the thought of Christmas shopping looming, darkness at 4.30 and frost and snow one should go at once to the first opening flowers of *Mahonia japonica*. Here one can be sure that in the garden, while everything passes, everything surely comes again; here an almost authentic whiff of lily of the valley can be sniffed every day until next April. From then it is only a week or two before the lilies of the valley themselves are out and we are well in to another spring.

List of Books Mentioned in the Text

Allen, David, *The Victorian Fern Craze*. Hutchinson, 1969.

Arnold Forster, W., *Shrubs for the Milder Counties*. Country Life, 1948.

Bean, W.J., *Trees and Shrubs Hardy in the British Isles*. John Murray, 1970.

Goodspeed, T.H., *Plant Hunters in the Andes*. N. Spearman, London, 1961.

Hillier, S., *Manual of Trees and Shrubs*. Hillier & Sons, Winchester.

Jekyll, Gertrude, *Wood and Garden*. London 1899.

Johnstone, G.H., *Asiatic Magnolias in Cultivation*. RHS, 1955.

Lloyd, Christopher, *Clematis*. Collins, 1977.

Moore, Thomas, *The Ferns of Great Britain and Ireland*, ed. J. Lindley, London, 1855.

Robinson, William, *The English Flower Garden*, 15th edn. John Murray, 1934.

Thomas, Graham S., *Perennial Garden Plants*. Dent, 1975.

Walter, Heinrich, *The Vegetation of the Earth*. English University Press, 1973.

Index

209

Index